Sean,

Keep Liberty Alive

Professor Sheldon

cMay 10, 2019

American Views of Liberty

Major Concepts in Politics and Political Theory

Garrett Ward Sheldon
General Editor

Vol. 5

PETER LANG
New York • Washington, D.C./Baltimore • Boston
Bern • Frankfurt am Main • Berlin • Vienna • Paris

Peter Augustine Lawler

American Views
of Liberty

PETER LANG
New York • Washington, D.C./Baltimore • Boston
Bern • Frankfurt am Main • Berlin • Vienna • Paris

Library of Congress Cataloging-in-Publication Data

Lawler, Peter Augustine.
American views of liberty / by Peter Augustine Lawler.
p. cm. — (Major concepts in politics and political theory; 5)
Includes bibliographical references and index.
1. Liberty. 2. Right and left (Political science). 3. Political science—United
States. I. Title. II. Series: Major concepts in politics
and political theory; vol. 5.
JC599.U5L37   323.44—dc21   97-8545
ISBN 0-8204-2412-9
ISSN 1059-3535

Die Deutsche Bibliothek-CIP-Einheitsaufnahme

Lawler, Peter Augustine:
American views of liberty / Peter Augustine Lawler. –New York;
Washington, D.C./Baltimore; Boston; Bern;
Frankfurt am Main; Berlin; Vienna; Paris: Lang.
(Major concepts in politics and political theory; Vol. 5)
ISBN 0-8204-2412-9

Cover design by James F. Brisson.

The paper in this book meets the guidelines for permanence and durability
of the Committee on Production Guidelines for Book Longevity
of the Council of Library Resources.

© 1997 Peter Lang Publishing, Inc., New York

Printed in the United States of America.

Contents

Introduction

The essays collected here present diverse views of the American understanding of liberty. One reason for the diversity is that I wrote them at different times and for a variety of purposes. Another reason is that human liberty is an incoherent mixture of diverse elements. It eludes definition or theoretical comprehension. Let me also warn the reader that I am writing this introduction years after I wrote most of these essays. I may understand what I wrote then better or worse now.

I begin, rather traditionally, with the Declaration of Independence, with the view that its understanding of liberty is the lens through which the Constitution should be interpreted. But my view of the Declaration is rather uncommon, even un-Jeffersonian. Contrary to the pretensions of Jefferson and other leading founders, it is far from free from Christian presuppositions. Most deeply, the Declaration defends the freedom of creatures to perform their duties to their Creator. Jefferson's own thought, I go on to show, provides insufficient guidance for the American search for a humanly worthy view of liberty. His most personal or private view of liberty was Epicurean, a thoughtful, pleasurable freedom from religious or superstitious hopes and fears. Jefferson understood well that this personal view of liberty, as both selfish and elitist, is quite deficient morally and politically. He claimed, quite unpersuasively, to have found the necessary democratic supplement, a natural foundation for the irrational benevolence of secularized Christianity.

The Jeffersonian combination of personal Epicureanism with support for moral and political inclination is found in the philosophic best-seller by Allan Bloom. For Bloom, too, human liberty is really the pleasurable freedom of a very few from all human illusion. It is the result of facing one's mortality straight on without flinching. But Bloom complains that the students he taught in the 1980s were actually free from any genuine awareness of their mortality, and so they were also free from human *eros* or love. The students' freedom might also be understood as a form of secularized Christianity; democratic therapy or history actually produced what the Christian God promised, freedom from death. Bloom's recommendations for the restoration of the twinship of love and death through the study of the Great Books is compromised by his philosophic elitism. He really agrees with the democratic therapist that most human beings would be better off not knowing they are going to die.

I also consider the views of liberty presented in three other recent best-sellers. Robert Bellah and his coauthors criticize the prevailing American view of liberty, "utilitarian individualism," for its selfishness and self-destructiveness. They agree with Bloom that contemporary Americans have been deprived of the language to articulate and so have difficulty experiencing the limits to their individualism, their love for and devotion to others. They echo Alexis de Tocqueville about the danger that individualism will transform American liberty into apathy. But their communitarian alternative is compromised by being excessively political, maddeningly abstract or vague, and too strictly egalitarian.

Dinesh D'Souza's muckraking classic exposes how illiberal most American higher education has become. Our professors have become irritating hypocrites. They demand intellectual liberty to deconstruct the foundations for its possibility. D'Souza aims to save intellectual liberty by supporting the few remaining genuine supporters of reason and revelation. But I add that we will have to look beyond Bloom and Jefferson to restore an adequate vision of liberal education.

Francis Fukuyama's book about the end of history disappointed just about everyone. Its view of the coming of universal and homogeneous liberty in America and an Americanized world seemed both humanly unworthy and incredible. Fukuyama, in truth, waffles about history's end. He does not follow the rigor of his mentor, Alexandre Kojève, who explained the end of history would have to be the end of human liberty. Our species would be free from its specifically human discontent to live just like the other animals, wholly determined by nature. Fukuyama, contrary to his intention, gives plenty of evidence that human liberty cannot be wholly secular or atheistic. It depends upon the distinctions that separate animal, human being, and God. Bloom, by describing Americans free of both God and death, actually seems more convinced than Fukuyama that history has ended.

Two of my essays concern the liberty of political leaders in America. The Constitution's framers aimed to make presidents constitutionalists, or to give them every incentive to limit and direct their exercise of power according to constitutional forms. By so doing, they would protect the people's liberty. But the framers knew that there would always be "leaders," those who oppose themselves to the limitations of constitutional forms on behalf of their own liberty. They hoped to discourage the president from being a leader, and to protect him from opposition leadership. George Bush's failed attempt to win reelection wholly without leadership is a case study in the limits of constitutionalism. Successful presidents are rarely, if ever, that conservative.

American conservatism tends to define itself against liberalism, and so it defends human liberty against the encroachments of government. But I explain that American conservatives have a variety of often conflicting views of what human liberty is. The libertarians, techno-optimists, Christians, traditionalists, paleoconservatives, neoconservatives, Straussians, and Thomists all share a devotion to virtue or personal responsibility, but they differ concerning virtue's true foundation and the conditions most conducive to its perpetuation. For prudent conservatives far more than utopian liberals, human liberty eludes theoretical determination and projects for social reform.

I conclude with Tocqueville, the most profound and elaborate of the modern writers supporting human liberty. He defends the American love of liberty against the twin dangers of the impersonal love of equality and the centralizing science of administration. The best Tocquevillian of our time, Walker Percy, echoes Tocqueville when he describes Americans restless and deranged in the absence of God. Tocqueville and Percy oppose, better than Bloom or Bellah, the therapeutic project to put death to death, and, in effect, to bring history or human liberty to an end. They say that, with some help, most human beings can live well enough in death's light. On that point, they agree with the Christians. I conclude where I began: The Americans' views of liberty depend upon Christian presuppositions, and perhaps on Christianity's truth.

Once again, I must give special thanks to Kathy Gann, who put this manuscript into shape for publication. I also thank Jocelyn Jones, Amanda Mullins, and Ryan Vila for their proofreading. Jocelyn also prepared the index. Rowman and Littlefield, *Modern Age*, *The Journal of General Education*, *Perspectives on Political Science*, *Presidential Studies Quarterly*, and *Gravitas* were all kind enough to allow me to reprint my work, sometimes in revised form. Generous funding from the Earhart Foundation gave me the time to bring these thoughts together.

This book is dedicated to Rita and Catherine, and their patience through it all.

Acknowledgments

"Theology and America's Liberal Democracy" originally appeared in *Modern Age* 31 (1987) and is reprinted with permission.

"Classical Ethics, Jefferson's Christian Epicureanism, and American Morality" originally appeared in *Perspectives on Political Science* 20 (1991). It is reprinted with permission of the Helen Dwight Reid Educational Foundation and was published by Heldref Publications, 1319 18th Street N.W., Washington, D.C. 20036-1802. Copyright 1991.

"Bloom's Idiosyncratic History of the University" originally appeared in *Teaching Political Science* 16 (1989). It is reprinted with permission of the Helen Dwight Reid Educational Foundation and was published by Heldref Publications. Copyright 1989.

"Reflections on Bloom and His Critics" originally appeared in *The Journal of General Education* 41 (1992). It is reprinted with permission of the Pennsylvania State University Press. Copyright 1992 by The Pennsylvania State University.

"The Problem of Democratic Individualism" originally appeared in the *University Bookman* (1987) and is reprinted with permission.

"Fukuyama versus the End of History" originally appeared in *After History*, ed. T. Burns and is reprinted with permission of Rowman and Littlefield Publishers. Copyright 1994.

"*The Federalist*'s Hostility to Leadership and the Crisis of the Contemporary Presidency" originally appeared in *Presidential Studies Quarterly* 17 (1987). Reprinted with permission of Center for the Study of the Presidency.

"The Constitutional Presidency of George Bush" originally appeared in *America Through the Looking Glass*, ed. R. Barrus and J. Eastby and is reprinted with permission of Rowman and Littlefield Publishers. Copyright 1994.

An earlier version of "In Search of American Conservatism" was published in *Gravitas* (1996) and is reprinted with permission.

Theology and America's Liberal Democracy

America is rightly called a liberal democracy. The majority rules, but the liberty of each individual is protected. The majority is not really free to do everything it pleases. It is limited by a standard which exists independently of what it wills at any particular moment. This standard is found in "the Laws of Nature and of Nature's God," the truth of which is "self-evident."

When an individual violates these laws, he does so only by denying the truth about himself to himself. He replaces thoughtful openness to nature's intelligibility with willful blindness concerning the limits of his own nature. By grounding the limits of government's and the individual's will in "Nature and Nature's God," the Declaration of Independence and implicitly the Constitution assert the truth of a "natural theology," an account of the relationships between man, God, and the universe. Knowledge of the truth of this theology is personally accessible to every human being.

The Declaration's natural theology is sometimes thought to be nothing more than an articulation of the Lockean-Jeffersonian account of Nature's God. What this God teaches cannot be known through the authority of revealed religion. It is known through the deduction of the consequences of one's own most candid experience, the one which reveals the truth about one's own natural condition to oneself. This experience is fearful anxiety for one's self-preservation in a hostile universe, one in which God does not care for individuals in particular and hence in which each individual must care for himself. The experience generates knowledge of rights, all of which are deducible from the right one has to decide how best to preserve oneself. On its basis, it is possible to conclude that the very idea of natural rights is incompatible with Christian teaching or Christian experience.

This extreme view does not consider that it may well be possible to revolt against the Christian tradition while retaining certain presuppositions derived from Christian experience. One could attempt to trace the Declaration's defense of individual liberty to Socrates, but only if one forgets that he claimed it only for himself and a very few others and viewed most human beings as chained to the "natural slavery" of a given political order. The Declaration's view that the individual's perception of self does not depend on the given political order and results in the discovery of a liberty which is both good for and equally possessed by all human beings is decisively biblical and Christian.

According to the biblical-Christian view, every human person is capable of leading himself away from the superficial distractions of political things to a perception of himself as he really is, independently of all political judgments. The goodness of the experience is guaranteed by the fact that it culminates in knowledge of a personal God, who knows me as I truly am. For the Christian, the authority of the political realm is limited by the knowledge of each person's transpolitical existence.

The experience of human dignity inherent in the discovery of natural rights cannot be accounted for on Lockean terms alone. It points to and ultimately depends on the Christian experience of personal transcendence. Christians discovered the experience of the dignity of the individual self or "person." As long as this experience is remembered, the individual cannot simply be understood as a "citizen," as a means to some political end.

Consider also that the theology of the Declaration of Independence is not exhausted by Locke's and Jefferson's "Nature's God." Two other references to God were added by its signers to Jefferson's original draft. The Declaration's signers asserted that they were "appealing to the Supreme Judge of the world for the Rectitude of our intentions." This "Supreme Judge" is the God of the Bible, the Christian God, who knows and judges the purity of the individual's heart. Such judgments right human error and provide the justice which rewards those who really intend to act justly and punishes those who merely appear to be just but who, in truth, are not.

Finally, the signers possessed "a firm reliance on the protection of Divine Providence." They believed that God cares for human beings and provides for their good. They surely did not believe that the correctness of their ideas or the justice of their cause would guarantee victory on the battlefield. Hence they must have believed that merely political victories are not necessarily genuine victories. There is a type of success higher and more substantial than political success. This conclusion stands in contrast to the Machiavellian foundation of Lockean thought.

The general assertion of the Declaration considered as a whole is that knowledge of "Nature's God" is not incompatible with the Christian belief in a personal, transpolitical God who cares for and rewards and punishes human beings, who are free to choose between good and evil. This assertion is strongly reminiscent of the "natural law" of medieval Christendom, which the Lockean "law of nature" was meant to replace.[1] The natural theology of the Declaration of Independence does not mean to replace Christian doctrine but to create an order which would allow the political realm to exist in a way consistent with the Christian idea of personal freedom.

The founding view of the goodness of liberty is more biblical than Socratic or Lockean. It is not Socratic because it does not make liberty dependent on the completion of the Socratic program of philosophic education. It is not Lockean because it does not understand political liberty fundamentally to be a means for the effective pursuit of power and wealth.

Consider that the argument for the protection of property in *Federalist* 10 and in Madison's thought as a whole also cannot be reduced to an economic or "technological" argument. The protection of property means the protection of everything which is genuinely one's own from political dominion. It means the protection of the transpolitical integrity of each human person. In his most comprehensive reflections, Madison claimed that property includes not only "that dominion which one man [justly] claims and exercises over the external things of the world." It also includes "[i]n its larger and juster meaning . . . everything to which a man may attach a value and have a right." The latter definition includes one's own opinions and what is "of peculiar value," one's own "religious opinions," those concerning one's duties to God. Madison went as far as to say that "[c]onscience is the most sacred of all property," because it is what is most one's own.[2]

Does not the possibility of and goodness of freedom of conscience ultimately presuppose the truth of the "medieval" opinion that it is possible for each human being to experience his transcendent dignity by knowing God's will? Does not the Madisonian understanding of liberty point to the "Thomistic" principle that each human being has the personal responsibility freely to seek the good? The acknowledgment that all human institutions ought to be designed to support this free, personal responsibility frees the Church, the academy, and the family from political control, because their existence is far more *for* this transcendent personal striving than is the merely political realm. It has been often remarked that the founding obsession with liberty was opposed to the Platonic-Aristotelian emphasis on political education for citizenship and statesmanship.

America's natural theology, to conclude, is not purely Lockean because no genuinely theological perspective can be. If it requires illumination from some premodern perspective, it is at least as plausible to search for the key source of illumination in Christianity rather than in Plato or Aristotle. This conclusion becomes even clearer when one sees the connection between the "democratic" views of moral and intellectual liberty in the American and the Christian traditions.

Those who deny that the Declaration's natural theology owes anything distinctive to Christianity might well accuse me of defending a position which concedes too much to the nihilistic charms of the positivism of contemporary social science. It is true that I must acknowledge that political scientist Robert Dahl is not wholly wrong when he asserts in his enormously influential *A Preface to Democratic Theory* that "the logic of natural rights seems to require a transcendental view in which the right is 'natural' because God directly or indirectly wills it." Consequently, "such an argument inevitably involves a variety of assumptions that at best are difficult and at worst impossible to prove to the satisfaction of anyone of positivist or skeptical predispositions."[3]

Dahl's general point seems to be that Lockean epistemology cannot support the American natural theology. For Locke and Dahl, freedom is freedom through skepticism. They deny that anyone can show that there is a natural or divine order which human beings can discover and which limits and directs personal and political choice. Each of them denies that it can be shown to him that he is limited by any will but his own.

Dahl's skepticism is evidence that the Cartesian-Lockean epistemological assertions have created an America in which almost every sophisticated person believes that natural theology is nothing more than the attempt to impose dogmatically one's own will upon a universe which, so far as human beings can tell, has no order or purpose of its own. The same sort of criticism which destroyed divine and aristocratic authority and brought into being liberal democracy is also capable of destroying the founding authority of liberal democracy. The creative possibilities of Locke's thought depended upon the plausibility of the "surface" or exoteric aspects of his teaching, which appealed to traditional prejudices. But the "naked essence" of Locke's thought, to use John Courtney Murray's phrase, which was aimed at allegedly Christian and Aristotelian hypocrisy, in time eventually worked to destroy Locke's own "judicious" hypocrisy.

Given this skeptical liberation from the dogmatism inherent in every assertion of natural or divine order, how can Dahl justify the limitation imposed on government by the idea of liberal democracy? For him, it is clear that, in the absence of self-evident natural or divine guidance, "political equality" becomes "an end to be maximized." He "lay[s] down" the "postulate that the goals of every adult citizen of the republic are to be accorded equal value in determining governmental policies."[4] It is the only postulate consistent with the absence of moral or political authority independent of the individual's idiosyncratic assertion.

The positivistic political scientist, then, also relies on a "self-evident truth." It is clear to him that what he asserts to be just or unjust or good or evil has no "cognitive" or other "objective" status. It is the product of the unique emotional requirements of his particular self. He knows that what is "evident" to him is not necessarily evident to others and that there is no compelling way of evaluating competing claims of moral or political "evidence." From a natural or "epistemological" perspective, all such claims are equally arbitrary.

Candid self-analysis reveals to the positivistic political scientist that he has not the authority to impose his evidence on others. His evidence is just as worthy or worthless as everyone else's, and government has no "objective" basis to give preference to one claim over another. Candid self-analysis in the skeptical absence of dogmatism causes one to limit one's will to oneself by negating any illusion one might have about one's own moral or political superiority.

Dahl's understanding of the purpose of government can be, and has been, criticized for denying the possibility of any public purpose and hence for reducing political life to the competition among separate but equal selfish forces or "interest groups." Given the atomism generated by its radical moral and epistemological skepticism, it is not even clear that it can explain how even an interest group can come into being. Its most fundamental problem, however, is its view of the experience of the individual. Each individual is free to assert without restraint the particular "goals" of his unique "self," but he has no foundation for justifying such assertions beyond this "self." Freedom through skepticism is freedom for the experience of the essential arbitrariness of one's own will through the recognition of the impossibility of a natural or any other form of theology. Dahl's individual encounters the experience of nihilism: everything is permitted because everything human is equally worthless or insignificant in the eyes of nature and God. God is dead, or He might as well be dead, because He has given to human beings nothing of any real value. Of necessity, we are all "self-made" men.

Does the candid, skeptical self really have the tendency to accept the limits imposed on it by the requirements of liberal democracy? Does it really tend to limit its will in view of its essential arbitrariness? Remember that Dahl argues that positivism and skepticism have destroyed the illusions of theology and natural rights. These illusions must have been human creations. Human selves must have been creating in response to human need. Apparently, human beings need to believe that there is some support for their humanity. Human dignity, they need to assert, must have a more secure foundation than human assertion. It must be more than purely self-created. This need, Dahl might conclude, is the foundation for the theological experience.

Skepticism or reason epistemologically understood destroys the credibility of such experience. But does it destroy the need for an understanding of human dignity that is grounded in a reality that exists beyond one's own self? If such a reality does not exist, ought I not attempt to create one by imposing my "goal" upon others, by creating a political reality that gives my assertion of dignity an existence beyond myself? Cannot the unsupported self desire to become a "godlike" tyrant, to create a world in its own image? Precisely because my assertion is arbitrary, and because I do not want it to be, I cannot rest content with the relativism of Dahl's liberal democracy.

But, Dahl might reply, political creations with arbitrary foundations do not, from a theological or natural perspective, really change the status of the "self." Candid self-analysis finally reveals the ultimate futility of all such efforts. Hence it should limit drastically what one ought to demand and expect from political life. But if I come to recognize both the indifference of God and nature to my particular existence and the futility of my self-sufficient striving to impose my will on my "environment," should I not conclude that human liberty itself is an evil? Is not liberty ultimately defined as liberty for genuine self-consciousness? If self-consciousness is nothing more than an experience of human worthlessness, does it not reveal my experience of myself as a human individual and as an evil to be destroyed? Does it not reveal the bankruptcy of the goal of liberal democracy?

Consider the two most powerful intellectual currents today calling for the destruction of liberal democracy, behaviorism and Marxism. According to the Marxist, liberal democracy or capitalism must be overcome by a final revolution which will bring history to an end. At the end of history human beings will be definitively satisfied. They will no longer experience the alienation or self-estrangement that the bourgeois man associates with self-consciousness.

Marx says this alienation, in truth, has an economic cause. Hence, when economic scarcity is definitively overcome for all human beings, everyone will be satisfied. Self-consciousness will become an experience of free self-realization unconstrained by any form of necessity and in harmony with the whole species. One will no longer experience oneself as an isolated, radically contingent individual. This terrible experience is merely a reflection of capitalism's economic individualism.

At the end of history, Marx acknowledges, human beings will still die, and they will be aware of it. There will not really be complete freedom from necessity, and one will still be able to differentiate one's own good from the species' good. It seems one will still experience oneself as an alienated individual. Although there will be plenty of "products," there will not really be enough from a perspective which is both self-conscious and materialistic. The ultimate scarcity is scarcity of time, and, as long as human beings are still both self-conscious and mortal, scarcity will continue and so will alienation. History cannot come to an end on a Marxian basis.

Perhaps Marx's vision can be salvaged with just a few alterations in the name of consistency. If human beings are called those who are both self-conscious and mortal, they must be called, by definition, unsatisfied or alienated. If the end of history produces satisfaction or the end of alienation, then those beings heretofore called human should properly be called something else. They become either gods or beasts. They are not gods, because a god is a being who is immortal. They must be beasts; they must lose that quality which makes human beings distinctive from a liberal or individualistic perspective—self-consciousness. If human beings were no longer aware of their mortality or radical contingency they would no longer be unhappy. They would be happy or, better, content, as we humans today call the animals content. If liberal democracy is to be overcome in the name of the end of history, the goal to be achieved is the elimination of self-consciousness, the abolition of man properly so-called.

This conclusion, of course, is explicitly affirmed by the behaviorist psychologist, who attempts to abolish freedom and dignity or humanity in the name of the survival and contentment of a certain type of organism. A moment's thought reveals that the goals of Marxism and behaviorism are essentially the same. Both aim at the creation of docile, cooperative "species beings" totally content with their environment. The enemy of this contentment is individualistic or human freedom.

There is a tendency today to view this destruction of individuality in a theological context. The movement is from the "privatization" of theology in the "bourgeois" perspective toward the comprehensive transformation of humanity as a whole envisioned by the "theology of liberation," which more or less equates the Marxist goal with the bringing of the Kingdom of God to earth. This liberation will involve the abolition of human suffering, all of which, having been man-made, can be eliminated by man. This liberation will eradicate all political distinctions, as well the ones between heaven and earth, the spiritual and the material, and man and God.

Apparently destruction of the Declaration's natural theology does not necessarily culminate in nihilism, because the "theology of liberation" shows that this destruction can be given a theological interpretation. Alexis de Tocqueville in his justly celebrated *Democracy in America* calls this interpretation "pantheism," and he calls its emergence the "principal effect on philosophy" of the democratic revolution in thought. As the "system" which most effectively destroys human individuality, pantheism portrays the completely homogeneous vision of the universe which is the foundation for purely democratic political idealism.[5] Tocqueville is able to see quite clearly and distinctly the journey democratic thought takes from liberal democracy to pure democracy. It ends with the affirmation of the truth of pantheism.

The revelation of the truth of pantheism is democracy's "ideal." So, it is, for Tocqueville, the key source of democratic "poetic inspiration." Every "philosophical system," every natural theology, for Tocqueville, is a form of poetry. Every vision of the universe which is not purely chaotic "ennobles" nature.

The democratic vision of the universe, from this perspective, is necessarily a "natural theology." Its skepticism prohibits the inclusion of "supernatural beings." Gods and heroes have been reduced to their merely natural proportions. Nothing beyond the visible and tangible world enters the democratic imagination. Democratic poetry "ennobles" what is "really" true from this democratic or homogeneous and materialistic perspective.

The destiny of "the human race as a whole" is the true democratic poetic vision. This destiny cannot be known to any particular individual. It is the product of human effort but not of individual choice. The democratic poet must conclude that the ordinary achievements of the individual find cosmic significance as part of an unknowable but "universal and consistent plan by which God guides mankind."[6]

The democratic poet, then, sees divine purpose in the growing success of the democratic movement and humanity's collective technological striving. All this success must have a point. That the point eludes the individual and apparently does not radically alter his human condition only shows the error of dwelling on the individual's perspective. At first glance, it makes sense to call this divine process "history" and to celebrate it as humanity's liberation of itself from the chains of natural necessity through its own efforts, as does the Marxist. But because history's divine goal is not chosen or even affirmed by human actors, human beings cannot truly say that historical success is a manifestation of human freedom.

The dualism between history and nature is also opposed to the democratic intellectual quest for comprehensive "unity," the most general of general ideas. More to the point, humanity will not really be free as long as this dualism exists. Human beings will still have bodies and die alone. They will still be individuals. Hence the genuine theology of liberation is not historical but pantheistic. The distinction between any form of human freedom and brute natural necessity must be eradicated. Brute, man, God, and inanimate nature must all become one. Human distinctiveness must completely disappear in order for one to see this vision of the perfectly democratic or perfectly homogeneous natural theology. The individual must see that his individuality is nothing but an illusion and will his own destruction in the name of the truth.

The affirmation of the truth of pantheism through the destruction of individuality or self-consciousness is the only "theological" doctrine which is perfectly compatible with the homogeneous and materialistic view of the universe implicit throughout the development of modern philosophy. Individualism or self-consciousness appears as a problematic exception to this general view, and the partisan of homogeneous materialism cannot explain it. He might attempt to explain it as an evolutionary product of the species' instinct for self-preservation. But this explanation is not very scientific, because the experience of history teaches the incompatibility between the consequences of self-consciousness and self-preservation.

The proper explanation of self-consciousness is as a mysterious "accident." No "theory of evolution" can satisfactorily account for the emergence of humanity. How and why humanity came to be is not known. From the perspective of homogeneous materialism, humanity is an "error," an example of "deviant behavior" about which the "scientific method" cannot give an account.

It is the task of science and scientific Enlightenment to replace error with truth. It is the task of science to eliminate humanity or self-consciousness. If it cannot, then science is not truly science. It is the project of science, of the enlightenment, to make homogeneous materialism wholly true. In so doing, it makes pantheism really true. A human individual is, for the homogeneous materialist, an animal who is for some inexplicable reason aware of his mortality and is dissatisfied with it. He is a beast who wishes to be a god and who can, to some extent, delude himself into thinking he really is godlike. The scientific destruction of humanity eliminates the characteristically human illusion that a human being is a being "in between" beast and God.

Without the existence of humanity, the distinction between beast and god also disappears. A being who lives in serene contentment, experiencing nothing but the sweet sentiment of its own existence, is simultaneously bestial and godlike. He is in need of nothing, so far as he knows, because he is not an individual in the Lockean or Christian or Socratic sense. He has no "historical" experience of his past, no "technological" concern for his future, no sense of his likeness to God, no curiosity about his cosmic status and the structure of the cosmos. He is divinely self-sufficient. For him, each moment is complete in himself and is completely satisfying. It is an experience of the truth of pantheism.[7]

Pantheism is the democratic remedy for the error inherent in the "naked essence" of Locke's anti-theological or materialistic individualism. For

Locke, the experience of Aristotelian-Christian-biblical natural theology, even as it is found in the Declaration of Independence, is an illusion. The idea of natural theology is generated by the experience of the world as one in which there is ample provision for the meeting of human needs. The crucial opinion, to repeat, is that there is support beyond one's own world for the individual's humanity. The world was created for beings made in the image and likeness of God. The truth of this opinion, moreover, is somehow self-evident to human beings, who use it to guide human choice.

For Locke, God and nature provide almost worthless materials. All that is given is formless matter which must be fashioned for human use by human labor. Human beings, once enlightened or freed from self-made illusions, can see only that nature is the source of all human dissatisfaction. The fundamental truth is human embodiment and hence human mortality. Human freedom is nothing but the mysterious existence of individual self-consciousness, which is fearful and uneasy, and reason, which is nothing but an instrument to direct labor in the interest of alleviating the pain produced by fear and uneasiness. Locke teaches the terrible necessity of this worldly self-reliance in candid acknowledgement of the absence of a God who provides for or even cares about the needs of individual human beings.

For Locke, the imagined existence of a natural theology created by human beings is simply additional evidence of their fundamental neediness, of the truth that no one has provided for them. It is this experience of fundamental neediness, this consciousness of mortality, that causes human beings to need a God who cares for them by satisfying the need for immortality. Yet, according to Locke, this need would be satisfied only if each human being were really immortal. If this were so, the distinction between man and God would disappear. Because man desires to be God, he imaginatively creates a God who gives him a godlike freedom from brute natural necessity. But, in reality, only if man were God would there be a God.

The Lockean analysis gives human beings no alternative but to make themselves as godlike as possible through their own labor. But this alternative is not a satisfactory one. Technological successes do not really bring freedom from fear through genuine individual security. In the best imaginable situation, death would be eradicated as a necessity, but not as a possibility, because it is impossible to eliminate all contingency from the infinite universe. In this situation, the place of fear in the individual's life would increase immeasurably. He would live in a lead house and never go outside. If death is avoidable, then all human effort must be concentrated on avoiding it. Courage and the other virtues become no longer the best ways of facing the necessary finitude of human existence, but insanity purely and simply. If death is avoidable, human life becomes pure misery, because there will never be any rest from the "technological" effort to avoid it.

The necessary failure of the Lockean project points to the truth of pantheism, which really seems to make human beings divine and relieves their human misery simply by eradicating their individuality or human distinctiveness. Pantheism makes manifest what Lockeanism only implies: the truth and goodness of the experience of human liberty cannot be shown by merely human beings.

This disappearance of the Lockean individual provides the crucial reason for suspecting that the experience of the truth and goodness of human liberty, at least democratically conceived, is decisively Christian. According to Vatican II's *Dignitatis Humanae*, "the right to religious freedom is based on the very dignity of the human person as known through the revealed world of God and by reason itself." Consequently, "freedom has its foundation not in the subjective attitude of the individual but in his very nature." Because the human person truly transcends the chains of political, social, and economic necessity by virtue of his nature, because he can know God and the good, human liberty really exists and is good for human beings.

Liberal democracy, understood in this light, has a genuine moral-religious foundation in its acknowledgment of the dignity and the transpolitical perfection of each human person. From this perspective, the political successes of the proponents of modern liberalism can be seen as genuinely good. Although they may have been inspired largely by the reductionistic "error" of Lockean materialism, they can be redeemed by the fact that the liberal end of this materialism may well have somehow (although ultimately incoherently) presupposed the truth of the Christian personal experience.[8]

Redeeming the democratic view of liberty requires inquiry into the nature of and the possibility of the truth of the distinctively Christian experience. This possibility is too often slighted or even ignored, even by those who seem to have the greatest desire to reinvigorate the idea of natural theology as the most effective antidote to the nihilism of the aimless relativism of positivism and of the ungrounded and hence unlimited assertiveness of historicism.

NOTES

1. For this distinction, see John Courtney Murray, *We Hold These Truths* (New York: Sheed and Ward, 1960), Chapter 13.

2. James Madison, "On Property," *The Writings of James Madison*, ed. G. Hunt (New York: G. P. Putnam, 1900–1910), 6: 101–03.

3. Robert Dahl, *A Preface to Democratic Theory* (Chicago: University of Chicago Press, 1956), p. 45.

4. *Ibid.*, p. 32.

5. See Alexis de Tocqueville, *Democracy in America*, trans. G. Lawrence (New York: Harper and Row, 1988), pp. 451–52 in the context of Volume 2, Part I, as a whole.

6. *Ibid.*, pp. 482–87.

7. See Jean-Jacques Rousseau, *Reveries of a Solitary Walker*, Walk 5.

8. See Walter Nicgorski, "Democracy and Moral-Religious Neutrality: American and Catholic Perspectives," *Communio* 9 (Winter 1982), pp. 292–320.

2

Classical Ethics, Jefferson's Christian Epicureanism, and American Morality

I want to discuss one reason for teaching the course usually called "Ancient and Medieval Political Philosophy" in American colleges and universities today. This course, as I understand it, involves the reading of some of the great moral and political philosophic texts from Plato to Thomas Aquinas. The authors read are those called classical and classically Christian. I want to show why this course is an indispensable ethical supplement for Americans to American political thought, one that is required for overcoming the moral crisis our democracy now faces. The beginning of this crisis is already present in the ethical doctrine of the most morally concerned and theoretically minded of our founders, Thomas Jefferson.

There is a rapidly developing consensus that we are now in the midst of a moral crisis and that its source is the diffusion of attitudes and opinions held by those responsible for higher education, our professors. Recent scholarly best-sellers such as *The Closing of the American Mind* by Allan Bloom, *Habits of the Heart* by Robert Bellah et al., *The Naked Public Square* by Richard John Neuhaus, and *After Virtue* by Alasdair MacIntyre agree that Americans are affirming more and more uncritically a sophisticated, easygoing moral relativism that is equivalent to moral nihilism. They also agree, in one way or another, that this moral nihilism originates in a denial of the credibility of the principles and beliefs that have shaped our tradition of moral education.

One undeniable benefit of the study of classical ethics today is the discovery that indifference to moral seriousness on behalf of freedom or personal choice is not a new phenomenon. It is, as Socrates explains in the *Republic*, a characteristic of extreme democracy wherever it exists. Celebration of the consistency of this extremism—given the pretentious name "anti-foundationalism"—is presented in some quarters today as the cutting edge of theoretical inquiry. This celebration is not of genuine innovation, but only of how democratic or relativistic America and the West have become.

The antidote to relativism, for Socrates, is moral education. The traditional American approach to this education is the recovery of the moral perspective of our founders, who seem to have had a worldly and progressive devotion to liberty without suffering from relativism or nihilism. Their perspective, in turn, seems to have been formed to a great extent by the classical philosophers and Christianity. Their debt seems clear in our founding documents, in which appeals to natural reason and revelation are both so prominent. The Declaration of Independence, for example, refers to both "Nature's God" and the Creator. Its theology is obviously some mixture of philosophy and Christianity.

But the character of the founders' intellectual debt is really quite problematic. The most powerful effect, it seems to me, of studying Plato, Aristotle, Augustine, Thomas Aquinas, and so forth is to show how incoherent and even unlivable a moral compromise the American mixture is. Our founders seem to have drawn freely from both classical and Christian thought without really accepting the most radical claims of either. The founding mixture lacks the sublime integrity and theoretical plausibility of either of its ingredients. The founders, finally, were moral partisans of neither reason nor revelation.

Jefferson's most private and theoretical reflections are the most decisive support for this conclusion.[1] Jefferson was indebted to modern writers such as Locke and Newton for his understanding of both political and natural science.[2] But his ethical debt, he says, was to the ancient philosophers and Christianity. It is sometimes said that Jefferson's selective interpretation of the New Testament is, at bottom, a product of the anti-Christian and anti-traditional skepticism of Enlightenment philosophy.[3] But he himself viewed it as genuine or "primitive," or not a philosophic interpretation at all.

Jefferson's most theoretical ethical reflections are found in a few of his letters, especially one to Doctor Benjamin Rush (21 April 1803), his friend and partner in theoretical conversation. To Rush, Jefferson had the best reasons for, and no fear whatsoever of, speaking his mind. Gone, for the moment, were merely political, including rhetorical, considerations.

This letter means to fulfill a promise Jefferson had made to Rush in the midst of some "delightful conversations," which were a respite from the political crisis of 1798–99. He gives his views on "the Christian religion," which, he says, are "the result of a lifetime of inquiry and reflection."

These thoughts have occupied his mind whenever he can "justifiably abstract" it "from public affairs" (to Rush, 21 April 1803). They are part of what always most delights him. Thought remains delightful even as the rest of life declines and becomes "wearisome" (to William Short, 31 October 1819).

The letter turns out to be a comparison of Christian and ancient philosophic ethics. Jefferson begins by denying the common opinion that he adheres to some "anti-Christian system." He asserts, in this most private and theoretical moment, "I am a Christian." He accepts "the genuine principles of Jesus himself." There is no feigning in this expression of conviction. Jefferson really believes that the "system of morals" of Jesus is "the most perfect and sublime that has ever been taught by man."

Jefferson's affirmation of Christian morality has nothing to do with the acceptance of divine revelation, especially Jesus's divinity. Nor does it have anything to do, necessarily, with man's duties to God. Jefferson affirms Jesus' and his moral doctrine's "human excellence" (to Rush, 21 April 1803). Jesus gives a better account than the philosophers of our duties to others, ones that we are inclined to perform by our natures.

Almost two decades later, in a letter explicitly meant to supplement the one to Rush, Jefferson adds, "I too am an Epicurian [*sic*]" (to Short, 31 October 1819). He explains that "Epictetus and Epicurus give laws for governing ourselves, Jesus a supplement of the duties and charities we owe to others." He had already written Rush that the greatness of ancient philosophers "related chiefly to ourselves," to how we might achieve "tranquility of mind" through "government of passions" (to Rush, 21 April 1803).

Jefferson's study of classical ethics led him to become a Christian Epicurean, or, more precisely, partly Christian and partly Epicurean.[4] Christianity is superior morally, because, for Jefferson, morality has nothing to do with self-love and everything to do with our duties to others. Nevertheless, the selfish teaching of Epicurus seems more fundamental. Jesus, Jefferson says, provided only a "supplement." Jefferson accepted the Epicurean account of natural necessity and the human condition as fundamentally true, which Jesus, in his simplicity if for no other reason, could not have done. Epicurus's atheistic materialism provides the basis for "the consolation of a sound philosophy, equally indifferent to hope and fear" (to Short, 31 October 1819).[5]

The difference between the ethics of the ancient philosophers and Jesus, as well as the insufficiency of either by itself to direct a fully human and moral life, is reflected in Jefferson's cautions about the corruptions of each. Ancient ethics is corrupted by "the idolatry and superstition of the vulgar." It is not meant for the vulgar, for most human beings. Jefferson's limited, but quite genuine, appreciation of its precepts, and his application of them in his own life, is one key point of distinction between his own and common opinion. His deepest opinions are, in part, undemocratic, which is one reason why they must remain private in a democracy (to Rush, 21 April 1803). The self-government or liberty in the precise sense of the philosophers is a life that is never lived by more than a few (to Mrs. Cosway, 12 October 1786).

Christianity is corrupted by the "learned," who serve their own "interest" by "perverting" its "simple doctrines" (to Rush, 21 April 1803). They turn "primitive" into "Platonizing" Christianity (to John Adams, 13 October 1813). The Christian system appeals to and is a reflection of the human being's "moral sense" or feeling, which is given by nature and has nothing to do with and is easily distorted by reason or calculation. Because it concerns our duties to others, and not to ourselves, it is emphatically not a philosophic doctrine.

The Christian system of morals is most powerfully threatened by the Socratic dictum that knowledge is virtue, which is used by the learned or clever to show that they are particularly virtuous and deserve to rule by reason of their virtue. Jefferson identifies this moral doctrine with the trickery of the sophists, which, for him, includes the mystifications of Plato (to Adams, 13 October 1813). But, most radically, he sees clearly enough that what threatens the simple truth of morality is the ancient philosopher's partly reasonable propensity to separate himself from the vulgar by reason of this thought. This propensity, of course, Jefferson himself shared.

The ancient philosophers, in their integrity, recommend a life of enlightened self-control and self-sufficiency, one that points away from benevolence toward others (to Mrs. Cosway, 21 October 1786). They taught, Jefferson says, friendship to their kind, and patriotism and justice to those who were not of their kind. The philosophers knew that patriotism and justice are qualities most human beings must have for political community to sustain itself. They also knew that that community's per-petuation was useful for their own happiness. Hence they "taught" or "inculcated" in non-philosophers within their political community those qualities, without really including them "within the circle of their benevolence" (to Rush, 21 April 1803).

The philosophers' teaching of moral and political virtue was part of their enlightened selfishness. They did not regard patriotism and justice as good for their own sakes. They did not teach as virtues, because they did not even regard as useful, "peace, charity, and love to our fellow men," the virtues that Jefferson regards as particularly democratic. The philosophers saw no reason to embrace "with benevolence the whole family of mankind" (to Rush, 21 April 1803).

Ancient philosophical ethics was selfish and elitist. It neglected what philosophers have in common with non-philosophers. On the individual's duty to others, Jefferson says, "it was short and defective." This defect comes, apparently, from an excess of reason. For Jefferson, Allan Bloom captures the perspective of the philosophers in its purity when he says that they, as philosophers, use morality and politics for their apolitical and amoral ends.[6]

Jefferson seems to rank the philosophers according to how free their "precepts" are from moralism and politics. His list of the "individuals" whose thought formed "the most esteemed of the sects of ancient philosophy" includes "Pythagoras, Socrates, Epicurus, Cicero, Epictetus, Seneca, and Antoninus" (to Rush, 21 April 1803). Conspicuous by their absence are Plato and Aristotle, the most political of the ancient philosophers. Plato, Jefferson says in his letter to Rush, "only used the name of Socrates to cover the whimsies of his own brain," which were, he adds in his Epicurean letter, "mysticisms incomprehensible to the human mind."

Plato is the least pure of the philosophers. Cicero is better than Plato, but too close to him. Evidence of Cicero's Platonism is his hypocritically moralistic attacks against Epicurus, in which the Stoics shared. Jefferson praises Seneca as less Stoic than most, and Epictetus is ranked still higher as the least Stoic of the Stoics. But it is in "the genuine . . . doctrines of Epicurus" that is found "everything rational in moral philosophy which Greece and Rome left us" (to Short, 31 October 1819). The least moral and political of the philosophers, the most openly selfish and materialistic of them, is the most rational, and the least hypocritical.

Epicurus's doctrine, because of its rationality and lack of moralism, exposes most clearly the partiality of the philosophers' ethics. Jefferson seems to have absorbed to some extent the Christian criticism, expressed, most eloquently, by Augustine, of the selfish and self-deceptive pride of the philosophers. But he does not agree with Augustine that there can be no justice without the loving subordination of the creature to the Creator. He also views any attempt to reconcile the morality of the philosophers with that of the Christians as Platonism, a doctrine that always promotes, in practice, something like the tyranny of priests.

Jefferson especially opposed, without even mentioning his name, the natural-law doctrine of Thomas Aquinas, which attempts to integrate reason and revelation by informing reason by revelation and revelation by reason. Jefferson agrees with Thomas without knowing it, and views himself as a Christian, because he holds that human beings have a natural inclination toward morality, toward performing their duties to others. The ancient philosophers, Jefferson recognized, discovered no such inclination. They regarded patriotism and even justice as conventional or political inculcations.

In Thomas's Christian correction of Aristotle, natural inclination and conscience (*synderesis*) replace, to some extent, moral-political education, and have a universalizing tendency on ethics. But for Thomas, nature intends these inclinations to be ordered and informed by reason. Morality is not primarily a matter of feeling, but of reason or prudence.[7] Thomas points to the integration, Jefferson to the radical separation, of natural moral inclination and reason.   .

Thomas also holds that the distinctively Christian virtues, the theological virtues, are "infused." They depend upon the grace of God, upon the human being's friendship with a God who cares about his or her existence and promises satisfaction of his or her deepest desires. Charity, for Thomas, cannot be a virtue for someone who accepts the Epicurean account of the human condition.[8] Thomas denies what Jefferson seems to believe, that there is a purely natural foundation for charity. In this respect, Thomas is closer to the ancient philosophers than to Jefferson. It is Jefferson's secularized, Christian faith in the goodness of nature that seems naive and ungrounded.

Jefferson's doctrine of "moral sense" or "conscience" or "moral instinct" describes what nature gives beings "destined for society." This instinct is the source of moral action, for it directs human beings toward and provides them with pleasure when they do their duty to others. There is a natural sensitivity to their suffering that "prompts us irresistibly to feel and succor their distresses." This instinct has nothing to do with "science" or perception of the truth. It also has nothing to do, contrary to Plato, with some appreciation of the beautiful. Because nature is so easily distorted by the "artificial rules" imposed by reason, "the ploughman" is more likely to act morally than "the professor" (to Peter Carr, 10 August 1787).

This understanding of moral sense or instinct seems to be Jefferson's main debt to the so-called Scottish Enlightenment. The term *moral sense* was first used the way Jefferson uses it by Francis Hutcheson, a professor of moral philosophy at the University of Glasgow. Hutcheson, like Jefferson, radically separated self-love from morality or benevolence or disinterested concern for others. Because the moral sense is an instinct, it owes nothing to reason, and it is not reducible by reason to something else.

Hutcheson radically separates morality from reason to save it from the materialistic or sensationalistic psychological reductionism of modern, especially Lockean, philosophy. Because reason had been revealed to be a slave of the passions, and incapable of directing human beings to some distinctive, moral end, the saving of morality required that it too be reduced to passion or instinct.[9] The selfish materialism that Hutcheson finds in modern philosophy Jefferson traced to ancient philosophy, or to philosophy understood properly at all times. Morality has to be separated from reason and become simply a feeling, because the life of reason is always a life of personal selfishness. There is no rational foundation for charity, benevolence, and so forth.

Hutcheson's moral doctrine, in its extreme form, was rejected by most of his contemporaries as incredible. They objected, especially, to the radical separation of morality and self-interest.[10] The location of moral action in some instinctive moral sense, somehow shared by all human beings but having nothing to do with reason, no doubt now seems incredible to us all. If morality is reduced simply to feeling, then it might come from any feeling or experience. The doctrine of moral sense is a very short distance from the easygoing moral relativism Bloom describes. The latter doctrine, of course, is more reasonable or plausible than the former.

There are other ways in which Jefferson fails to ground properly the moral foundation of the American republic. It is usually described as a liberal democracy, a regime in which the majority rules but minority rights are protected. Its premise is that democracy and liberty are harmonious or interrelated goods, that they are not, fundamentally, at odds.

But, for Jefferson, it seems that Epicurus was a liberal, and Jesus was a democrat. Their doctrines were quite different and, from the perspective of their originators, incompatible. Jefferson claims to be, by reason, a liberal and, by instinct or "heart," a democrat. The least that must be said is that this personal combination is quite fortuitous. The ancient philosophers, after all, were full of reason. But, according to Jefferson, that is why they were deficient in moral instinct. He criticizes them for being too liberal and undemocratic.

Liberty, for Jefferson, means a private or personal freedom from the claims of common opinion for one's own self-government. It is the freedom he claims in communicating theoretically and privately to Rush. Rational, personal cultivation, what the ancient philosophers called cultivation of the soul, is possible only for the very few. For this cultivation only, the study of the ancient philosophers is of the greatest use. Jefferson's love of classical learning was not, as Eva Brann claims, a "noble and baseless preference,"[11] but a personal and pleasant or "delightful" one. Thomas Jefferson, Epicurean, might say that it is an amoral but well or philosophically grounded preference.

The study of "moral philosophy" Jefferson added, is "lost time" (to Carr, 10 August 1787), because there is, strictly speaking, no such thing. Morality must be democratic or common, because all human beings are social. It must be rooted in sense or instinct, and not in reason, because most human beings are not philosophers or scientists. They are not particularly reasonable or knowledgeable, but nature intends them no less than philosophers to act socially or morally. The study of morality, with or by professors, can only distort or mystify the simple "sentiment" of moral goodness (to Mrs. Cosway, 12 October 1786).

As Brann notes, "[n]either God nor the good . . . were . . . intended to be preoccupations" in the "republican university" designed by Mr. Jefferson.[12] The deepest reason for their absence, it seems to me, is there is no reason, no argument for one's attachment to and practice of the democratic or Christian virtues. Nothing could be more wrongheaded in Jefferson's view than a project to reinvigorate American morality through the study of the ethical texts that constitute our tradition. For Jefferson, the moral sense can be strengthened only through its exercise, not its study (to Carr, 10 August 1787).

But it is clear to us that Jefferson's revulsion against the ethical selfishness of the ancient philosophers was not really a product of his simple feelings, however well exercised they were. It owes a good deal to the universalism of reason, as he must have learned from the Stoics, as well as to the Christian criticism of the pagan philosophers' hypocritical elitism. But Jefferson differs from the philosophers in not finding in their rationalism the source of moral doctrine, and from the Christians in denying the truth of revelation. It seems that he reduced his moral revulsion to feelings because he denied the integrity and plausibility of his moral sources. What he has reduced to feelings, remember, is his devotion to democracy.

The superficiality and incredibility of this reductionism, this doctrine of moral instinct, leads us, against Jefferson's intention, to Augustine and Thomas Aquinas. They show us, with greater plausibility, why human beings might see charity, in opposition to the teaching of the philosophers, as a virtue. It is only lately, in response to an elitist or libertarian project to create what Neuhaus calls a "naked public square," that the concern has become widespread that America's devotion to democracy might depend upon our devotion to the biblical-Christian understanding of the person. The project Neuhaus describes is a perversion of Jefferson's understanding of classical ethics. The antidote he recommends is stronger than devotion to the doctrine of Jefferson's secularized Jesus.[13]

It may be, as John Courtney Murray asserted a generation ago in *We Hold These Truths*, that only some form of Thomistic natural law can articulate credibly our founding principles.[14] Jefferson's warning against pursuing that possibility concerning the tyranny of priests seemed credible in his time, but rather remote in ours. Natural law, as Neuhaus recognizes, is also an antidote to fundamentalism, the moral doctrine of which is rather close to Jefferson's in its denigration of the place of reason.

The insufficiency of Jefferson's separation of reason and feeling also leads us, against his intention, to Plato and Aristotle. His view was that all philosophers, when they are not being hypocritically and fancifully moralistic, are Epicureans. All philosophers are either open or closet Epicureans. This Jeffersonian opinion is not at all superficial. Nor is it one generally thought to be incredible today. Will Morrisey, for example, has suggested that Allan Bloom never said enough to show why he is not an

Epicurean.[15] He often presents himself as, above all, devoted to philosophical *eros* or pleasure, and he attributes Epicurean views to Socrates.

But Plato and Aristotle transformed the world by giving guidance to political life that at least seems to be spiritual and not moralistic or tyrannical. Their doctrine survived the ravages of time precisely because it did not reduce all existence to matter, because it did justice to the longings of the human soul. They held that reason can understand and guide moral and political life, and that political philosophy is not simply the use of politics by apolitical philosophy.[16] Jefferson, surely, was more of a Platonist than he knew. The inspiration of the Declaration of Independence is not that of a partly Christian and partly Epicurean author.

The inability of our professors to educate morally is largely rooted in their acceptance of Jefferson's doctrine. They follow Jefferson in separating reason and morality, reducing moral judgment to feeling. Remarkably like Jefferson, they are uncritically attached to the virtue of compassion, which is plainly a selective, secularized, and incoherent interpretation of the Christian virtue of charity. Our professors often acknowledge that the virtues they prefer have no real foundation, that the truth, from reason's perspective, is technocratic selfishness and moral relativism.

Jefferson's view that professorial Platonism is a dangerous tyrannical impulse remains at the heart of the doctrine of anti-foundationalist professors of philosophy such as Richard Rorty.[17] From the perspective of Jefferson and Rorty, any moral turn to classical or classically Christian ethics is profoundly subversive of democracy. But Rorty's view is, as we have seen, challenged by another opinion among critics today, one I think is more reasonable. It is that our moral crisis is somehow rooted in the relativistic excesses of democracy. We have lost the moral foundation of liberal democracy, which is somehow rooted in reason and revelation. We blame our professors, in effect, for not being Platonic enough. But to engage in moral education to counter the excesses of democracy on democracy's behalf, they have to look beyond Jefferson and the American founding.

Jefferson was neither a relativist nor a moral nihilist. He seems distant from our moral crisis. But his ethical doctrine's superficiality and incredibility does lead to our professors' view that morality has no foundation. His partly Christian and partly Epicurean ethics at first seems to reflect the tension between reason and revelation that, according to Leo Strauss, is the secret to the West's vitality. But that appearance, too, is deceiving. Jefferson really dissolves the tension by not taking the moral claims of either reason or revelation seriously enough. He says that neither is really the source of morality.

But liberal democracy really does depend upon the vitality of that tension. Its liberty or limitation upon government does depend upon our perception of the moral goodness of the transpolitical lives of the philosopher and the saint. Its liberty understood democratically depends upon Christianity's universalization of the transpolitical experience of liberty, one that the ancient philosophers, and even their contemporary disciples such as Bloom, believe is available only to the few—the imitators of Socrates.

NOTES

1. All the letters referred to in the text can be found in *The Life and Selected Writings of Thomas Jefferson*, ed. A. Koch and W. Peden (New York: The Modern Library, 1944).

2. See Sanford Kessler, "Jefferson's Rational Religion," *The Constitutional Polity*, ed. S. Pearson (Lanham, MD: University Press of America, 1983), pp. 58–78.

3. Kessler uses a letter of Jefferson's to Rush (16 January 1811) as evidence that he was primarily a partisan of modern philosophy, a Lockean (p. 69). There Jefferson writes that "Bacon, Newton, and Locke . . . were my trinity of the three greatest men the world has ever produced." But this is hardly evidence that Jefferson was convinced of the superiority of their moral doctrine. He seems to have held that the philosophers and scientists, ancient and modern, are, in their way, the greatest of human beings, but they are still deficient morally. Kessler also takes the obvious fact that Jefferson was not an orthodox Christian as evidence that his thought was not influenced by Christianity at all, that he was a rational man, a philosopher. This conclusion, according to Jefferson himself, is far too simple and, in its way, morally obtuse. The Jefferson that Kessler seems to admire John Gueguen criticizes. Gueguen calls Jefferson's doctrine "anthropocentric neo-paganism," calling attention to his "explicit disavowal of the central tenets of Christianity (in an 1819 letter to William Short)" ("Modernity in the American Ideology," *Independent Journal of Philosophy* 4 [1980], p. 86). The letter to which Gueguen refers is Jefferson's Epicurean letter, where he says that the doctrine of "sound philosophy" needs to be supplemented by the morality of Christianity. If "neo-pagan" means a simple return to the doctrine of the ancient philosophers, then it does not describe Jefferson's moral doctrine. If it is the mixture of Christianity that puts the "neo" in neo-pagan, then Gueguen is on the mark.

4. A comparatively early expression of this division is found in Jefferson's dialogue between head and heart, between "science" and

"sentiment," in his letter to Mrs. Cosway (12 October 1786). Chaninah Maschler sees with unrivaled clarity that this argument between head and heart is really between apolitical ancient philosophy and Christianity ("Some Thoughts About Eva Brann's *Paradoxes of Education in a Republic,*" *Interpretation: A Journal of Political Philosophy* 10 [January 1982], p. 127).

5. In a letter to John Adams (15 August 1820), Jefferson identifies the genuine teaching of Jesus with a sort of theistic materialism. He calls "immaterialism" a Platonizing "heresy" with atheistic implications. It is obvious to Jefferson that only matter exists. Those sophisticated individuals who say that God is not, in some sense, matter are really saying that he does not exist. A simple Christian, he seems to say, would not think to distinguish between the material and some other world. But Jefferson, at the end of his letter to Rush, praises Jesus for introducing "the doctrine of a future state" as an important supplementary moral "incentive."

6. See Charles R. Kesler's instructive criticism of this aspect of Bloom's *The Closing* in his "The Closing of the American Mind: An Instant Classic Reconsidered," *Essays on the Closing of the American Mind*, ed. Robert L. Stone (Chicago: Chicago Review Press, 1989), p. 175.

7. See especially Thomas Aquinas, *Summa Theologiae* I, question 79, articles 12–13 with I–II, question 94, articles 1–6.

8. Thomas Aquinas, *Summa* II–II, question 56 with question 65.

9. See Frank Balog, "The Scottish Enlightenment and the Liberal Political Tradition," *Confronting the Constitution*, ed. A. Bloom (Washington, D.C.: AEI Press, 1990), pp. 196–98 for a very concise and precise summary of Hutcheson's moral doctrine. Balog does not make the connection with Jefferson. But see Maschler, p. 126.

10. Balog, pp. 198–99.

11. Eva Brann, *Paradoxes of Education in a Republic* (Chicago: University of Chicago Press, 1979), p. 86.

12. *Ibid.*, p. 92.

13. On Neuhaus, see my "Thoughts on Neuhaus's 'Catholic Moment'," *Political Science Reviewer* 17 (1988).

14. On Murray, see my "Murray's Natural-Law Articulation of the American Proposition," *John Courtney Murray and the American Civil Conversation*, ed. R. Hunt and K. Grasso (Grand Rapids: William B. Eerdmans, 1992).

15. Will Morrisey, "How Bloom Did It: Rhetoric and Principle in *The Closing of the American Mind*," Stone, p. 60.

16. See Alexis de Tocqueville, *Democracy in America*, trans. G. Lawrence (New York: Harper & Row, 1988), p. 545.

17. See Richard Rorty, "Straussianism, Democracy and Allan Bloom I: That Old Time Philosophy," Stone, pp. 94–103.

Bloom's Idiosyncratic History of the University

I want to discuss one chapter of Allan Bloom's *The Closing of the American Mind* (Simon and Schuster, 1987), his "idiosyncratic history of the university" (312). I do so with the intention of opening the next stage of analysis about this extraordinarily provocative and instructive book. It has already sparked a huge amount of contentious writing, much of which has been intelligent and illuminating. But almost all of it has been in the form of reviews, however extended. Critics have attempted to assess the book as a whole without considering sufficiently its parts. They have, in other words, attempted the impossible, as reviewers must do.

Bloom's book, although quite accessible, is extremely dense, both in terms of argument and information. It is also written for many purposes. It has a polemical surface, defending liberty understood as philosophy, and delicate and ironic depths, which cause the thoughtful and careful reader to question that which Bloom seems to hold most dear. Now that the immediate furor surrounding the controversial best seller has subsided, it is possible to engage in textual commentary to expose the radicality of the book as philosophy. Its genuine radicality is its exposure of the question-ableness of philosophy.

Bloom seems to present his "idiosyncratic history" as an almost self-sufficient whole. As history, it is almost Hegelian in its comprehensiveness, an intelligible story with a beginning, middle and end. It is also the history of human wisdom understood as the relationship between human self-consciousness or individuality and human community or politics and culture. The chapter which presents this history is entitled "From Socrates's *Apology* to Heidegger's *Rektoratsrede*." In it Bloom understands Heidegger to have attempted, with at least considerable success, to deconstruct what Socrates (or at least the author of the *Apology*) constructed. The history of the university is the history of political philosophy, which Socrates opens and Heidegger brings to a close. It is not clear whether the history is progress toward or away from wisdom. It is not clear, in other words, who is wiser, Socrates or Heidegger. There is plenty of irony in this lack of clarity.

Bloom's history of the university is an "idiosyncratic" one for many reasons. For him, this history is *the* history of the West, as well as *the* vindication of the West's essential superiority. He is not very interested in the university's development as an institution. From his description, one would not know the historical fact that the university as an institution originated in medieval times, because he understands those times, in their Christian conviction, to have been hostile toward philosophy. Bloom's interest is the history of the university's spirit or soul. Socrates, he says, is this soul.

Bloom says that the university begins in spirit with Socrates's contemptuous, personal opposition to Athens, his partisanship on behalf of his truthful experience against political error. For Socrates, all political communities are fraudulent. They exist, most fundamentally, to cover over the fact that the existence of particular human beings has no "cosmic" significance. Human beings are self-conscious mortals who exist as individuals apart from their attachments and commitments. The philosopher as philosopher constantly confronts his mortality. He does not lose this awareness in his attachment or devotion to others or in his pious belief in providential gods or God or in a deceptive feeling of self-sufficiency produced by pride, courage, or nobility.

For Bloom's Socrates, the only truly human existence is in the light of this wisdom, which results in freedom *from* the gods and other illusions *for* the desire to know the truth about the nature of all things. Bloom's Socrates pursues wisdom because in the decisive sense he is already wise. What separates him from other human beings is that wisdom. Ignorance is not so much a matter of lack of intelligence as the reluctance to confront the truth about one's particular existence, which, perhaps, in the absence of fear of death, would be easy for human beings to know. Wisdom is hard only because passion closes the mind to what it can know.

Bloom says that philosophy has nothing to do with the virtue of honesty. But he also makes it clear that the philosopher is the only genuinely honest human being. By defining the experience of philosophy as knowing or confronting continually the truth about one's own mortality or particularity, Bloom seems to identify philosophy with the contemporary doctrine of existentialism, a set of opinions with which his sophisticated audience would already be familiar and would find quite plausible. By making the truth seem easy to understand, at least for citizens of a permissive, "enlightened" democracy, Bloom makes the affirmation of the experience of the philosopher seem more akin to moral than intellectual virtue.

Yet Bloom also says that the philosopher as philosopher does not practice moral virtue. Our world must be unusually friendly to philosophy for Bloom to write so openly about the philosopher's experience and its ability to destroy the credibility or weightiness of other human experiences, especially those associated with the virtues flowing from love of family, God, and country. In Bloom's mind, what clearly separates his book from others about the experience of the philosopher is this openness or candor. Is this openness inseparable from moral decadence or relativism? Does Bloom complain *because* he can write so plainly? But he is not, as a philosopher, a moralist.

What separates the Socratic philosopher from the existentialist intellectual or even the existentialist philosopher is that he experiences knowledge of the truth to be the most profound human pleasure. The pain or anxiety that accompanies genuine self-awareness is more than compensated for by the pleasure of "insight." It is the experience of this pleasure, and hence of the goodness of the truth, that is the ultimate justification of the university. It is an experience that non-philosophers do not ordinarily have. They escape from the truth to piety or a pretentious sense of self-sufficiency or the "everydayness" of communal involvement.

Most human beings, the non-philosophers, cannot really see why the university or genuinely liberal education is good. The political community cannot really affirm the goodness of the university and the human experience it most fundamentally promotes. Hence, Socrates did not think that a university, a publicly supported and respected institution animated by his spirit, is possible. That thought, more than anything else, separated him from the philosophers of the Enlightenment. Nevertheless, they were animated by the philosophic or Socratic experience to become the true founders of the university.

Socrates's wisdom detaches him from moral and political concerns. From his lofty perspective, all such attachments look pretty much the same. Bourgeois, aristocratic, and religious culture and politics are alike in their fraudulence, in their hatred of wisdom. The philosopher as philosopher chooses among them, when he must involve himself in political life, on the basis of which is best for him. He supports one set of lies instead of another as a result of his calculation concerning which of them, under a given set of circumstances, protects and promotes his particular way of life.

The philosopher must be a deceiver, because he, in truth, opposes the illusions that support non-philosophic conceptions of human dignity and community. He does not mind lying to and otherwise using non-philoso-phers because he does not view them as good in themselves, as open to the truth. The moral and political "mind," as such, is "closed." Bloom does say that biblical moral tradition is somehow deeper or more noble than contemporary technocratic relativism. But it is also false, he makes clear enough, in its portrayal of man under God. The relativist, it seems, is closer to the truth.

Only the possibility of ranking moral and political "values" in terms of their usefulness for philosophy, which is essentially neither moral nor political, saves Bloom from affirming the truth of the deadly, relativistic distinction between facts and values, the one which his book was seemingly written to oppose. The only good is wisdom and its genuine pursuit. All things moral and political are, in themselves, no good. The philosopher as philosopher, even more to the point, says that human beings, insofar as they are unphilosophic or unwise, are no good. It would seem that the philosopher must be wise, and not merely in pursuit of wisdom, to affirm with certainty such an apparently ignoble, impious, and perhaps even misanthropic or nihilistic conclusion.

Bloom presents Socrates as having a certain consciousness of the superiority of his way of life to all other ways. Socrates's apparent uncertainty on the crucial human question is nothing but irony, because he did not live indecisively. He rejects decisively the cases that revelation might bring against reason or politics might bring against philosophy. Bloom and his Socrates do not, one might say, appear to be at all open-minded. They are, to repeat, in the decisive sense wise men. An open-minded person is not wise. If the philosopher were close-minded and not wise, then he would be a moralist or dogmatist. Bloom says that wisdom does not dissolve all community. It creates the community of philosophers, those who love or are friendly toward wisdom. What makes this commu-nity a community is not at all clear. It is held together most fundamentally not by the common pursuit of wisdom, it would seem, but by a common possession of wisdom, the truth about the significance of human mortality. It is the community of genuinely self-conscious mortals.

But the wisdom the philosophers have in common seems to point to their separateness. Each philosopher knows the full significance of the fact—he or she will die alone. Does not any perception of community distract one from that fact? Bloom sometimes identifies this community with the pursuit of scientific progress. But how could scientific progress of one sort or another change the fundamental wisdom philosophers already have? Would not, as Pascal contends, scientific investigation be an example of distraction or self-forgetting, a negation of wisdom?

Perhaps the community of philosophers is, in truth, held together by a common pride in the fact that philosophers do not share in the self-deceptive ignorance of others. But is not this pride, or consciousness of superiority, also rather self-deceptive? The philosopher seems to know that human pride is groundless, and hence pretentious.

According to a more common interpretation, what makes one a political or Socratic philosopher is not one's awareness of the truth about death as such but the conviction that the life of the mind leads, somehow, to the true conception of the good in common. Why is the truth about death, as Bloom presents it, such a good? To put the question another way, why is the university, Socratically understood, either good or possible?

This question points to the philosophers who conceived and conspired to carry out the project called the Enlightenment. According to Bloom, the unity that is the Western tradition comes from the fact that these philosophers agreed with Socrates about the truth and goodness of the experience of the philosopher. They conspired to change the world on behalf of this experience, to make those who have it no longer hated, but publicly respected and even dominant. Philosophers would, in their publicly-funded universities, be free to think and experience what they please.

These philosophers wanted more than to be left alone with their experience, simply to avoid the fate of Socrates. They wanted their leisure, to be free, as far as possible, from the constraints of "earning a living." They had to rule, it seems, in order to secure this freedom. But ruling, for Socratics, is unphilosophic, and hence unfree. It is, Socrates says in the *Republic*, an unpleasant and time-consuming necessity. In the name of freedom understood as unfettered leisure, the philosophers surrendered their apolitical freedom and entered seriously political life.

The Enlightenment philosophers, Bloom asserts, took seriously politics and its derivatives like culture without really caring about them at all.

They meant to use them for their purposes without being distorted by them. They attempted to rule through deception with a clear conscience, or no conscience at all.

Non-philosophers or non-scientists were seduced into Enlightenment, and thus into accepting its core institution of the unfettered university. They were led to believe that their lives would be improved by the resulting progress of science. The element of deception or seduction, at first glance, is unclear. It would seem that their lives were improved, and they came to live in liberal democracies (the best example of which is the United States) longer, more comfortably, and more freely.

But, Bloom adds, with what seems to be a repulsive candor, the philosophers did not care about any such improvement in non-philosophic life. He says that the original intent of Enlightenment liberalism and its meaning of the doctrine of rights was to give philosophers or scientists a right to free inquiry. Any "democratization" of that meaning to include some non-philosophic liberty of conscience or expression, or simply a generalized freedom from tyranny, is a distortion. The authors of *The Federalist*, Bloom asserts in particular, did not care about religious liberty for the sake of religion. Their partisanship on behalf of diversity was not on behalf of ways of life not devoted to reason. It was, in truth, only intended to keep the unwise from being able to direct effectively against the wise their inevitable animosity toward the truth. Devotion to diversity was to mean, in practice, deference to wisdom through control of passion.

Bloom goes on to show more indirectly that the Enlightenment philosophers knew that they were not, in the decisive sense, improving the lives of non-philosophers. They knew they could not truly "enlighten" non-philosophers or bring them out of the cave. They actually meant to deprive non-philosophers of their souls, to create "bourgeois" individuals.

Such a miserable, contemptible individual spends all his time calculating how best to preserve himself comfortably. He calculates constantly about the rest of his life on the basis of his fear about violent or premature death. He forgets that no matter how effective his plans may be, he remains mortal. He becomes, in a way, a reasonable or science-dependent being only because he never reflects upon and hence never rebels with passionate animosity against the invincible limits to human existence. He does not fight for or even hope for immortality, because, unlike the philosopher, he never encounters eternity.

The Enlightenment philosophers, in their sham charity, created the political context in which humankind might experience the fruits of the unlimited progress of science. To accept them without reservation, human beings had to suppress the longings of souls. They surrendered the pious perception that such progress would not transform their existence fundamentally. This perception, for Bloom, is compatible with Socratic wisdom, or the knowledge of the futility of all human projects in the light of eternity. Science might show human beings how to avoid violent death and how to die comfortably and peacefully at an unprecedentedly old age, but it cannot show them how to avoid death altogether, or even how to come to terms with its reality.

Faith in the progress of science implies an absence of *scientia*, or a knowledge of the way things really are. Bloom's argument that the Enlightenment philosophers, most fundamentally, did not have this faith is meant to save them from the theologically or poetically inspired charge that they were optimistic or superficial rationalists. They knew that human existence could not change.

Bloom says the Enlightenment was not superficial. It was rooted in the Socratic experience he holds to be most radical or most true. The philosophers of the Enlightenment did not hope to be understood. By institutionalizing a fraudulent faith in the goodness of wisdom, they made the proponents of philosophy or wisdom more vulnerable in many respects than they had been "in the closet" as part of a rebellious, clandestine enterprise. Most human beings, by their natures, revolt against wisdom, and hence against the university's purpose, when they see it for what it truly is and for what it truly can do to what they hold most dear.

Although the spirit of the university may be Socratic, Bloom admits that very few Socratic types have ever found a home there. For Bloom, good professors, for some non-philosophic reason, respect or look up to what they cannot be. Some sincerely respect wisdom and devote their lives to it, but even that devotion is based on a misunderstanding. Those scientists who make the fundamental contributions to scientific progress usually do not truly understand the significance of their activity for their own existence. In Bloom's terminology, it seems that philosophers, not scientists, confront squarely their own mortality. Scientists forget themselves in their devotion to theory, to the impersonal materialism which generates science's progress.

Bloom asserts that the practical intentions of the Enlightenment philosophers had little or no theoretical significance. On the key issues, they were Socratics. But much of his evidence points to the conclusion that the practical decision, in fact, led to or was the product of theoretical changes. His reader cannot help but suspect that the Enlightenment philosophers disagreed theoretically with Socrates.

Bloom's deepest opinion might even be that the Enlightenment was caused by some un-Socratic theoretical distortion. There must be something un-Socratic in his eyes about the Enlightenment philosophers' decision to institutionalize scientific progress and the rule of scientists. It must be more than merely a strategy to produce philosophic leisure. The Enlightenment interest in such things *is* a diversion, in Pascal's sense, from wisdom or the truth about human existence.

Bloom says that as the Enlightenment developed it experienced not only practical but theoretical crises. The attempts to resolve these crises always took the form of more rigorously or radically identifying human freedom not with wisdom about mortality but with human "creativity." The progress of science itself became identified with this freedom. The scientist does not discover but creates. Creativity becomes inseparable from knowledge.

This understanding of freedom Bloom does not identify with the Enlightenment's original intention. Yet we cannot help but wonder about that conclusion. From Leo Strauss, Bloom learned that Machiavelli was recognized by the philosophers as the real founder of the Enlightenment or modernity. Machiavelli, Bloom says, was motivated largely by "anti-theological ire" and not by anger against Socrates or the philosophic experience. Machiavelli was a philosopher, a lover of wisdom, just like Socrates.

Machiavelli, not without reason, hated the practical effects of Christian theology, and he did not hate Socrates. These conclusions can be accepted as true without forgetting, as Bloom seems to want us to do, that Machiavelli, in one decisive sense, lumped Socrates and his school with the theologians. Machiavelli, unlike Socrates, affirms the "vulgar" conclusion that the truth is the "effective truth." He affirms the theoretical conclusion that the truth must be proven to be true through empirical experimentation. Philosophers prove theory to be true through their "creativity," through their use of it to change the world. The modern university, Bloom says, identifies reason and "competence." The wise person is necessarily a competent one. But Socrates's wisdom—his knowledge about death—in Bloom's eyes would not seem in any automatic sense to lead to competence. It would almost seem to preclude it.

The modern or Enlightenment dispute with Socrates here is epistemological. How does Socrates know he is wise, that the experience of the philosopher is true? How is philosophy to be distinguished from insanity? The philosopher, according to Socrates, appears, unadorned, to most other human beings and to any moral or political community, as insane. The only way, it seems, that the philosopher could decisively overcome this "common sense" objection to his experience is to change or "rationalize" and hence "deracinate" morality, religion, and politics on its basis. This overcoming is impossible, Bloom quite reasonably says. No Machiavellian project can, in the decisive sense, succeed. Contrary to Hegel, the "real" cannot become the "rational." Because genuine Enlightenment is impossible, the experience of the philosopher remains questionable or, as Bloom says, "idiosyncratic."

In this light, Enlightenment comes to be seen, as Swift predicted, as the tyranny of philosophers. Philosophers become tyrants, or "creators," because they deny Socratic wisdom. Somehow in their freedom, they create in opposition to their human mortality or limitations.

The university, conceived as an Enlightenment product, as somehow built on a Machiavellian as well as Socratic foundation, is not in many respects devoted to Socrates's spirit. Its freedom of inquiry is not, even on the deepest level, designed to produce Socratic detachment. It is for the progress of science defined as technology, for changing the world, for enlarging human freedom defined as creativity. It is so not only for practical reasons, to satisfy its non-philosophic supporters, but also for theoretical ones. Scientists or philosophers want to rule, it turns out, because they want to know. From Socrates's perspective, they identify knowing with ruling because they are denying wisdom, or diverting themselves from it quite self-consciously.

Bloom gives us enough evidence to suspect that the Enlightenment's unfettered university does not exist for Socrates. It is, in many respects, not even animated by his spirit. Its existence is distorted not only practically but theoretically by its political origin. The idea that the university is for detached, Socratic pursuit of wisdom is part of its propaganda, a deliberate exaggeration of the extent to which modern theory can be apolitical or untyrannical.

Bloom engages in this propaganda himself. He often asserts, despite the evidence to the contrary, that the university is at its core apolitical or detached from moral concerns. He even asserts that Nietzsche, apparently a great partisan of the will and creativity, disagrees with Socrates in a Socratic way. But, in truth, Nietzsche rejected the Socratic account of the philosophic experience as intrinsically the most pleasurable for human beings and productive of the only genuine human community.

For Nietzsche, what Bloom calls the philosophic experience is the terror of the abyss, the nothingness that surrounds arbitrary or accidental human existence. Wisdom is terrifying and misery-producing, and, if defined as the core of human existence, produces the conclusion that human existence is no good. The Socratic account of it is superficial and misleading. He does not, in truth, come to terms with the full significance of truth about human existence.

For Nietzsche, Socrates shares the superficial optimism of the Enlightenment philosophers. As Bloom says, Nietzsche's claim, *the* radically modern claim to wisdom or "insight," is historicism, the view that one's perception of the truth is determined inevitably by time and place. Thought does not transcend but is dependent upon history and culture. At first glance, historicism seems to mean that there is no human wisdom detached from historical context.

But, for Nietzsche, that is surely not the case. The human perception of the abyss or the groundlessness of human existence is always true. Perhaps a human being might perceive it as true at any time. It is always the human propensity to create order or "culture" or "meaning" in opposition to that experience. Human existence is created in response, consciously or unconsciously, to the discovery of groundlessness.

There is, in truth, no "community of philosophers" that somehow transcends political or cultural life. There is no content or ground for human distinctiveness to be discovered. The university, as an institution and hence a community, is radically dependent on the creation of political or cultural context. Heidegger was right. There is no abstract "intellectual freedom" which somehow generates a curriculum and a community.

Socrates, then, was theoretically superficial if he truly thought that a radical encounter with the full significance of the truth about human mortality by itself can be the foundation of either human pleasure or community. By itself, it terrifies and isolates. Historicism means that there is no truth to be discovered, and hence that there is no Socratic good in common. In the decisive sense, it means that beyond the fundamental awareness of groundlessness, there is no genuine progress toward *scientia*. Faith in scientific objectivity is simply self-forgetfulness, a lack of courage to confront the truth about oneself. The philosopher or scientist, when he does not forget himself, experiences himself as a creator, one who imposes himself on the world in ultimately futile opposition to his mortality.

Enlightenment, from the perspective of Nietzsche's radically modern insight, is dogmatic. The dogma of its university is the Socratic account of the philosophic experience. Yet the Enlightenment philosophers also reject this dogma, and point toward Nietzsche's insight. They, beginning with Machiavelli, progressively more unreservedly and explicitly identify theoretical truth with the effective truth or history or creativity. The Enlightenment is some combination of a theoretical affirmation and a theoretical undermining of the Socratic experience in which the undermining is progressively more effective because it is more true.

Bloom suggests that the Enlightenment gradually exposed the university to be a philosophic prejudice. Yet he shares this prejudice quite consciously. He knows that the Socratic experience, by itself, cannot generate or animate a community. He also knows that one logical culmination of the Enlightenment is socialist or National Socialist revolution against Socratic self-consciousness. The Nietzschean will opposes the deadliness of truth on behalf of life.

Both the Left and the Right today, Bloom shows, are Nietzschean or Heideggerian. Marxism, in its metaphysical depths which Marx himself could not articulate, opposes Enlightenment. The revolution against "bourgeois" individuality is, in truth, against self-consciousness or the Socratic experience. Socrates, by dispelling human hopes and convictions, revealed human individuality to be the misery-producing illusion. At the end of history, Marx, the Hegelian, says, there will be no philosophy, only wisdom. Human beings will be content with their existence because they will have destroyed the miserable untruth of individuality.

Perhaps the end of history is here, Bloom also suggests, and without revolution. It is the closing or completion of the American or Western mind. Today's "nice" students who cannot take the university or anything else seriously claim to be wise, and without any effort. In their wisdom, they claim to see or experience no need for further thought or action.

Today's students seem to have accepted Socrates's destruction of the credibility of every way of life but his own, and to have become more Socratic than Socrates by applying his method to his life, too. Socratic seriousness is as illusory and misery-producing as every other form. (The students' "philosopher," we must add, is the self-consciously unserious Richard Rorty.)

Today's students, in the name of truth and contentment, refuse to devote themselves to a university animated by Socrates's spirit. They treat Bloom and Socrates with condescension, and all Bloom can do is bemoan their "flat souled" lack of seriousness. Their "erotic" experiences are superficial, because they are so astoundingly unself-conscious. They are not "sublime," but they do not long for what they cannot have. Their constriction of passion is in accord with their wisdom, an anti-human wisdom.

Bloom's analysis indirectly but insistently suggests the question-ableness of his "idiosyncratic" account of the university, not only from a historical, but a human, perspective. His account of its soul seems, in several respects, misanthropic. In its candor, it does—and is probably meant to—repulse morally and politically serious human beings. It makes clear that by itself, philosophy is not, in its uncaring "elitism," at the foundation of liberal *democracy*. Democracy, and liberty understood democratically, must have some other foundation, one Bloom has not articulated.

An open mind, surely, is one open to the questionableness of the experience of the philosopher. The Enlightenment philosophers, and even Bloom's Socrates, had insufficiently open minds. Does Bloom himself lack openness and is he acknowledging it?

The most profound criticisms of the philosopher's experience, those given by Christian thinkers such as Augustine and Pascal, are not consid-ered seriously by Bloom. He does not do so, apparently, as part of his personal or philosophic partisanship, though, to his credit, he has said much to suggest their plausibility. They are conspicuous in his book by their absence, as is any evidence of his reading the Bible as he says it should be read, "with the gravity of a potential believer." Reason can point the way to the necessity of revelation for human beings, even if it cannot bow to it.

The philosopher, as philosopher, cannot reinvigorate moral and political life. But he can acknowledge, as Bloom does, that the erotic openness or longing that leads to philosophy does depend upon that vigor. Even the university, in truth, depends upon un-Socratic elements that Bloom, from his idiosyncratic perspective, chooses not to articulate.

4

Reflections on Bloom and His Critics

Allan Bloom's wonderfully unlikely best-seller, *The Closing of the American Mind*, is far less an expression of America's, Socrates's, or even Bloom's mind or soul than it seems.[1] Every page (almost every paragraph) is informed by the thought and writing of Leo Strauss, whom Bloom regards as the greatest thinker of the century. For Bloom, the choice is between Strauss and Heidegger, the century's other great thinker. When Bloom attacks Heidegger as Socrates's great adversary and as the source of much of America's evil, he sides not so much with Socrates as with Strauss.

Bloom is a very derivative thinker, a fact that, admittedly, would not be known by a reader of *The Closing of the American Mind* who knew nothing else of Bloom, and nothing of Strauss. This fact, Bloom would quickly say, is neither good nor bad in itself. The key question is whether what Bloom learned from Strauss and the great thinkers he called to his attention in a certain way is true or false. One of Bloom's most solid observations is that far too much is made of creativity or originality in our time.

Strauss's thought has had some significant success in America. Its influence grows, although slowly. Some of those whom Strauss has most influenced, often called "Straussians," are prominent in both academic and political life. Under President Reagan, they were a subject of fascination as they became directly involved in the formation of public policy. They are often, but not always, known for their competence and circumspection.

The Straussians do not really form an ideological or sectarian whole. Their disputes with one another are not merely over details. They disagree, often with considerable animosity, over many of the issues that now shape American political life. They are both Democrat and Republican, pro-choice and pro-life, for and against affirmative action, and so forth.[2] They know, at least in their calmer moments, that their disagreements are perfectly understandable. According to Strauss, the human questions are always far more obvious than their answers, which always remain elusive. The experience of certainty required to affirm any particular answer inevitably involves some anger or animosity; it is not simply the product of reason.

The most spirited and profound criticisms of Bloom's book have been written by Straussians. They dominate Robert L. Stone's fascinating collection of 62 outstanding responses to *The Closing of the American Mind*.[3] They are best situated to understand what Bloom was attempting to accomplish. They also have the most reason to be concerned if he did not do so well. Most of them say, not surprisingly, that Bloom did not succeed in articulating the full complexity of human life. Some Straussian writers—most notably Harvey Mansfield, Jr.—brilliantly defend Bloom from well-known, but quite unfair, critics. But even Mansfield's defense of Bloom's argument is also an attempt to improve upon it.[4]

Bloom writes as a teacher, and mostly for teachers. He says he is a teacher far more than a scholar. Even as a scholar, he is attracted, above all, to the best books on education. His most noteworthy scholarly accomplishments have been his translations of and commentaries on Plato's *Republic* and Rousseau's *Emile*, for him *the* best ancient and modern books on education. No one who has studied with Bloom and written about his book denies his greatness as a teacher. But there are some who have important reservations about his scholarship and more who question his political judgment. Bloom may be a great educator, but even his Straussian admirers see that his wisdom is not perfect.

Bloom writes, as a teacher should, full of passion on behalf of the truth and against prejudice or illusion. He holds that teachers should oppose, most forcefully, the most powerful prejudices of their time, even those that have had beneficial effects. For example, what comes forth very powerfully from his book is his severe questioning of feminist individualism. His appreciation of the good that it has done is far more muted. Following Rousseau and Plato, Bloom is a critic of Enlightenment in the service of genuine enlightenment. But some of his critics wonder whether his questioning is too severe, whether he cares enough for what is politically beneficial. More than one calls attention to the manifest inadequacy of his political defense of the American founding, of the salutary devotion Americans have to the principles that shape their lives.[5]

Most of Bloom's critics begin with the allegation of elitism. This beginning is perhaps the least radical and courageous one. It is *the* conventional one, the one most in accord with the most powerful prejudices of our time. Democratic intellectuals, characteristically, view their task as the destruction of distinctions or "privileges." They immediately strike out against any assertion of authority or excellence as an illegitimate claim to rule.

Bloom's most interesting democratic critic, Richard Rorty, writes against the seriousness or intensity of his claims for philosophizing.[6] Devotion to philosophy or anything else gives no one, not even Socrates, Heidegger, or Bloom, the right not to be a relativist. All human assertions are without foundation. Rorty's relativism or anti-foundationalism passes, in some quarters, as the cutting edge of contemporary thought. In a sense it is: It is the democratic extremism described by Socrates in the *Republic*.

The charge of elitism against Bloom is usually made in a fairly thoughtless or chauvinistic way. Still, Bloom's Straussian critics take it quite seriously. They recognize it as the decisive criticism of Bloom. They see the urgent need to defend Bloom and good government against it. By so doing, they are defending themselves and a healthy political life. The charge, unrefuted, makes them suspicious in our democracy, far more suspicious than they deserve to be. Most of Bloom's Straussian critics also see that the charge, properly reformulated, has some truth to it. The fact that democratic opinion is our prejudice does not make it wholly untrue.

To begin with the refutation, Bloom's elitist opposition to radical or pure or relativistic democracy is not necessarily antidemocratic. It might be, as his book's subtitle suggests, a warning about America's democratic future. In the *Republic*, democracy is a prelude to tyranny. Democracy is too nice or lacking in devotion to defend itself from its enemies. There is nothing, in particular, to stop strong and passionate relativists from dominating weak and passive ones. Tyranny and relativistic democracy share the same view about morality: It is nothing but an arbitrary imposition.

Surely a democracy cannot be understood to be so easygoing as to be indifferent to its own self-preservation. Criticism of democratic extremism can be friendly criticism in the interest of democracy's perpetuation. The American founders were such critics. They were, to use Mansfield's judicious phrase, "responsible democrat[s]."[7] They did not hesitate to take responsibility for democracy's future.

Surely all forms of human community and government have their characteristic self-destructive excesses. It is an act of some courage to be on guard against the excesses of one's own. The greatest enemy a democracy has is not the self-proclaimed elitist, but the demagogue—the flatterer of the people. The demagogue always asserts that the prudent reconciliation of democracy and good government is at the people's expense. Our suspicions should be redirected once we realize that Bloom does not flatter, but most of his most vehement critics do.

A well-functioning democracy is necessarily concerned with excellence. Even Bloom, in Harry Jaffa's view, does not see the extent to which the American founders were both democrats and aristocrats in the precise sense.[8] According to Jefferson, for example, the best political order is one in which the people, in their virtue, choose the natural *aristoi* to rule.

Jefferson's radical opposition to conventional aristocracy, to the arbitrary rule of monarchs and priests, points neither to mass democracy nor aimless relativism but to a world in which excellence is impartially cultivated, suitably recognized, and combined with power. As Jaffa remarks, it is devotion to this world, as the ideal or goal of political striving, that more than anything else distinguished classical political philosophy in Strauss's mind. But for the democratic relativist, the very assertion that human excellence exists has no foundation. This antielitism flatters those who are lacking in all pretensions except for the distinctiveness one receives from debunking the distinctiveness of others.

The idea of equality of opportunity to distinguish oneself, the idea that democracy and aristocracy can be reconciled, has always been a popular one in America—although without, of course, the explicit reference to aristocracy. (Jefferson's reference was in a private letter.) The idea's popularity, Bloom holds, is threatened by higher education and the diffusion of its influence throughout America's cultural life. That education tends to diminish the citizen's uncritical devotion to Jeffersonian aristocratic democracy and to make him or her more consistently relativistic.

The many, it turns out, are less consistently democratic than the few. Radical antielitism or egalitarianism is the doctrine of those who define themselves by their devotion to ideas, the intellectuals. Intellectuals, in our democracy as in Socrates's, devote themselves to the destruction of inegalitarian distinctions. They do so in the name of the truth, but also in the name of dignity and happiness. The anxiety and restlessness that characterize competitive, individualistic, or somewhat undemocratic democracy produce misery and degradation. That the losers in this race of life are miserable in their poverty seems obvious. But even the winners are uneasy and otherwise discontented. Democratic intellectuals inherit, as intellectuals, the classical and biblical view that it is inhuman to be excessively concerned with money and power.

Bloom, of course, shares this moral opposition to the vulgarity of bourgeois life. But, he adds, it must be made clear that it is an objection to democracy. The people, in truth, aspire to be bourgeois. Intellectuals, in truth, reject both the popular and bourgeois standards with their devotion to ideas and idealism. The many will never share fully their devotion, nor their view of human excellence.

With the class interest of intellectuals *as* intellectuals clearly in mind, Bloom claims to be less antibourgeois or antidemocratic than most contemporary intellectuals. His criticism of democracy is part of a criticism of political community as such. All forms, democracy, aristocracy, and the others, are necessarily limited in their openness. No political community could ever really share Socrates's devotion. The life of the mind never really acquires political recognition.

Socrates could not be an exemplary citizen anywhere. Bloom's criticism of political life on behalf of the individual—or at least one kind of individual—puts him far closer to the democratic relativist than it first seems. The danger, which he recognizes, is that philosophical devotion too readily produces political relativism. Bloom's strongest critics are "conservative" antirelativists of various sorts, who are far more attached to the undemocratic or moral features of the American political community than he is.

Bloom's relationship to relativistic democracy turns out to be complex and ambivalent. Socrates, Bloom learned from Strauss, was not nearly as opposed to democracy as is usually supposed. The limitations of democracy were clear to him, as we have seen. It is indifferent to all forms of human excellence and even to its own self-preservation. It is also ugly in its willful refusal to confront the limits of human existence.

But unlike other political communities, radical or relativistic democracy, in its lack of devotion or passion, exhibits no hostility to the philosopher's quest for liberated thought through radical questioning. Only in a relativistic democracy (in contrast to the relatively serious or pious, devoted democracy of the Athenians) can the meddlesome Socrates live wholly without legal problems. Only in the openness and variety permitted by a democracy can a frank discussion of moral and political alternatives such as the one portrayed in the *Republic* take place. Only for a relativistic audience can Bloom write so plainly. His art of writing, for better and worse, reflects very little fear of persecution.

Bloom understands the relativism of American democracy to have been the product of his class interest. It is the creation of the conspiracy of philosophers called the Enlightenment. Using a certain sort of propaganda, they worked to undermine popular animosity against free thought and free thinkers. They created the bourgeois or materialistic, pedestrian world in which philosophers, posing as technologists, could find places on the public payroll. The world, as a result of Enlightenment, becomes progressively more democratic. Qualitative or soul-based distinctions, as Marx noted, lose their weight.

Bloom's criticism of relativistic democracy is similar to that of Marxists with aesthetic or spiritual pretensions, those who attempt to ennoble Marxism with strong doses from Nietzsche and Heidegger. He shows that the Left and Right stand together in opposition to the ugliness of American democracy. Philosophers and intellectuals, generally, are not nearly as happy in the bourgeois world as the Enlightenment philosophers thought they would be. The exploitation of non-philosophers by the Enlightenment philosophers, like all exploitation, turns out to have been bad for the exploiters.

The sixties best-seller that most closely corresponds to Bloom's is Herbert Marcuse's *One Dimensional Man*. Both Bloom's friends, particularly Timothy Fuller, and his enemies have noted the similarity of his cultural and sociological analysis to Marcuse's.[9] Both Bloom and Marcuse criticize, from the perspective of *eros*, the superficial or repressive conformity of bourgeois culture. Despite their political differences, it is impossible not to notice their common indebtedness to, fascination with, and dislike of Heidegger.

Bloom and Marcuse both set the requirements of civilization against *eros*. They take the side of what civilization, especially our civilization, regards as perversion. For Bloom, the highest or most passionate form of perversion is called philosophy, the one that is most extremely hostile toward and threatens most radically civilized order. He exhibits this hostility by describing philosophy as childish or irresponsible play, very close to the way the more openly antinomian Marcuse describes the activity of liberated eroticism.

For the most part, Bloom hides the radicality of this opposition to moral and political order by identifying civilization with the university, and the university with Socrates. But he also acknowledges that very few Socratic types have ever felt at home in such an institution. The claim that the university has ever really existed primarily for Socrates seems incredible, partly because all Bloom really claims is that the university means to be animated by the spirit of Socrates.

With his privileging of philosophy, Bloom does part company with Marcuse. Marcuse's promotion of multifaceted erotic gratification is meant to suppress the misery of human self-consciousness and, in its way, to conquer death. But Bloom holds that the pleasure accompanying the most extreme self-consciousness or "insight" into the place of human existence in the whole is the most intense one, one which more than compensates for the misery that accompanies self-conscious mortality.

Bloom at times also seems very distant from Marcuse in his moralistic rhetoric against sexual promiscuity. But all he favors is the subordination or sublimation of that easygoing, mechanical satisfaction to the pursuit of more profound longings and deeper satisfaction. Bloom often writes as if the cultivation of erotic longing is good for its own sake. By seeming to make *eros* an end, Bloom is again close to Marcuse, and far from moralists of every sort.

What really ought to attract and repulse us is not Bloom's moralism, which, he admits, is not for the sake of morality, but his eroticism. One of his Straussian critics, Pamela Proietti, is particularly disturbed by the "eerie and empty quality" of his "celebration of '*eros*.'"[10] She wonders whether it decisively undercuts the argument he seems to give for familial responsibility and the other requirements of civilized decency. She also wonders whether the radical liberation of *eros* could possibly be good for women and children.

Education, or at least higher education, is for Bloom the arousal and cultivation of the longing human beings have to escape from the constraints of ordinary human life. Michael Zuckert describes Bloom's understanding of education as "a passion-driven ascent from what the philosopher Martin Heidegger calls the sphere of 'average every-dayness'." This ascent, Zuckert goes on, has two motivations. The first is "discontent and restlessness." The second is the erotic or "positive desire for 'complete-ness.'"[11]

The negative experience of discontent seems good only because it is accompanied by the positive desire. More than Bloom acknowledges, bourgeois society's tendency to stifle the negative experience is based upon its hidden conviction or metaphysical presupposition that the positive desire cannot be fulfilled. Human discontent and restlessness, as Pascal held, produce nothing but distinctively human misery.

Bourgeois democracy must suppress the most profound human longings because it seems all too clear in times of Enlightenment that they cannot be satisfied. It must, for its own good, oppose the education Bloom promotes. Human life is never more (in Bloom's phrase) "flat souled" or (in Marcuse's) "one dimensional" than it is in bourgeois society. Zuckert's invocation of Heidegger to describe Bloom's view of education rightly connects Bloom, theoretically, with Heidegger's antibourgeois extremism.

The cause of the democratic, bourgeois world, Bloom says in one way and Heidegger in another, is the philosopher's effort to transform the world in the service of thought. The world so created turns out to be a disaster for thought and hence for higher education. The Nazi Heidegger entered the political or cultural world for a moment to save it from the extreme consequences of that transformation. His experience seems to have taught him that only a god can save.

For Bloom, Heidegger's project, allegedly in the service of humanity, was actually misanthropic or nihilistic in its extreme hostility to the philosopher's liberated or deracinated thought. It was, in a subtle sense, too democratic. A way Bloom might be guilty of elitism in a pernicious sense would be in his choice of liberated thought over what is required for human beings to live a happy, dignified life.

But Will Morrisey, perhaps Bloom's most astute Straussian defender, says that the denial that there is a radical conflict between liberated thought and human life is at the heart of Bloom's thought.[12] For Socrates and Bloom, knowledge, really self-knowledge, is more pleasurable than miserable. They avoid misanthropy or nihilism. *Eros* overcomes misery; it does not quite conquer, but at least compensates for, death.

But if it were not for that experience of intense pleasure, human beings would do well not to face straight on the miserable truth about their mortality. Bloom must conclude that nihilism is true in most cases, because the intense pleasure of insight is so rarely experienced. Most human beings, most of the time, do and should choose life over truth.

Bloom's hope for reform is in the university, and even there it is not very great. As some of his Straussian critics remark, he probably should have located it in the college, perhaps even the private, sectarian college.[13] The university cannot help but be dominated by the needs of bourgeois society. The college, however, is free, due to democracy's relativistic indifference to its existence, to stand in largely impotent opposition. At this point it seems that Bloom is so elitist that he, unlike Heidegger, poses no threat to democracy.

Bloom's indifference to democracy is not reflected, as some of his critics think, in his attitude toward the sixties. The "student movement" was, in its way, elitist. As Bloom shows, it met with little opposition from professors. It was decisively defeated not by any elite, but by Nixon's "silent majority," and later Reagan's "moral majority." It brought into being what is now called conservative populism. Majoritarianism, to repeat, opposed the intellectual project of radical egalitarianism.

Some critics, including the Straussian George Anastaplo, say that Bloom ought to show more sympathy for the longing reflected in the students' antibourgeois idealism.[14] Tom Hayden, in his response to Bloom, endorses the critical idealism of Great Books education and the greatness of classical philosophy.[15] But perhaps Bloom does show some implicit sympathy for men like Hayden, as Charles Kesler suspects, by failing to show any gratitude to or personal kinship with their effective democratic adversaries.[16]

Bloom seems to like the eighties much less than the sixties. He characterizes the spirit of the sixties as thoughtless indignation. This characterization, as Anastaplo observes, perhaps suits the situation Bloom faced as a professor at Cornell, but it is far too strong as a generalization. It does not seem to fit well cases such as Hayden.

The eighties, for Bloom, seem to have neither thought nor indignation. Hostility to Bloom and his ideas from students has been replaced by their indifference, which is surely more inhuman. Bloom sees no moral or intellectual truth in Reagan revivalism, and he is silent on various Strauss-inspired efforts to reinvigorate American democracy. Conservative populists—or conservatives who have become populists in the hope of directing democracy—can find little if any support in Bloom's book.

Neither can more refined cultural conservatives; Bloom finds so little in American culture worth conserving.

Bloom's seeming indifference to everything but the future of philosophy is surely a pose, an apolitical one. No concrete human being is exclusively a philosopher. Political philosophy is the attempt to articulate, in the soul of the philosopher, the conflict between his devotion to his own, including his political devotion, and his longing for the truth. Bloom reduces political philosophy to the use of politics for philosophy. It goes without saying that such an understanding is extremely undemocratic. But it is also, even from Strauss's perspective, overly simple. By not showing us the whole, complex soul of the political philosopher, Bloom has not shown us what political philosophy is.

Some readers contend that Bloom reveals more of himself than it first seems. Anastaplo goes as far as to say that "there are in *Closing* vibrations of one tormented soul." He sees in Bloom's soul a "curious blending . . . of *longing* and *anger*,"[17] which shows itself in his irrational or unphilosophic overreaction to the rebellion of the sixties. That personal reaction might be accounted for as an all too human exception to Bloom's Socratic rule.

William Marty, writing as a partisan of revealed religion, explains that the reaction is not an exception at all.[18] He notices that Bloom displays indignation whenever he discusses challenges, especially religious ones, to the claims he makes for philosophy. He strikes out against those such as Max Weber who say that our history or life has not been determined by a philosophic project. He, as the liberal Straussians Anastaplo and William Galston complain, unrealistically downplays the effects of social, political, and economic (not to mention religious) causation.[19]

Bloom says that indignation is the way human beings suppress doubt. Perhaps his anger causes him, as Eva Brann complains, to make too much of what distinguishes philosophers from non-philosophers. He denies that most human beings are reflective enough to benefit truly from liberal education. But according to Brann, they share the "roots of reflection"[20] with the philosopher. The philosopher also shares their doubt, indignation, and need for faith. As both his friends and enemies note, Bloom's analysis is singularly lacking in compassion. He seems to claim, quite unconvincingly, that he is beyond any need for it. Bloom's anger really does cause him to be less democratic than he ought to be.

NOTES

1. Allan Bloom, *The Closing of the American Mind* (New York: Simon and Schuster, 1987).

   One reason for the success of *The Closing* is given by the philosopher-novelist Walker Percy, "I think that the title has a lot to do with it. You go to a bookstore in a small town in Louisiana and see the damn thing piled up. It turns out that a lot of parents are buying it for their kids in college. It struck a nerve with parents who think that those damn professors are screwing up their kids."

   Percy's own view is that Bloom's book does not provide the cure that parents are seeking: "He covers his tracks very well. I suspect he is a nihilist" (Scott Walker, "Nuns, Nazis, and the Poor Old Pope: An Interview with Walker Percy," *Crisis* 7 [July/August 1989], p. 16).

2. Liberal Straussians include William Galston and George Anastaplo, both of whom will be discussed below. Galston is a leading force in the "neoliberal" think-tank the Progressive Policy Institute. He is a key advisor to Bill Clinton, and served on President Clinton's staff. A Straussian book with very liberal constitutional implications is Sotirios Barber, *On What the Constitution Means* (Baltimore: Johns Hopkins University Press, 1984).

3. Robert S. Stone, ed., *Essays on the Closing of the American Mind* (Chicago: Chicago Review Press, 1989).

4. Harvey C. Mansfield, Jr., "Straussianism, Democracy, and the Great Books" Stone, pp. 106–12.

5. See, for example, Harry V. Jaffa, "Humanizing Certainties and Impoverishing Doubts: A Critique of *The Closing of the American Mind*," Stone, pp. 129–53.

6. Richard Rorty, "Straussianism, Democracy, and Allan Bloom I: That Old Time Philosophy," Stone, pp. 94–103.

7. Mansfield, p. 109.

8. Jaffa, p. 134.

9. Timothy Fuller, "The Vocation of the University and the Uses of the Past: Reflections on Bloom and Hirsch," Stone, pp. 333–37.

10. Pamela Proietti, "American Feminists versus Allan Bloom," Stone, p. 218.

11. Michael Zuckert, "Two Cheers (At Least) for Allan Bloom," Stone, p. 75.

12. Will Morrisey, "How Bloom Did It: Rhetoric and Principle in *The Closing of the American Mind*," Stone, pp. 51–60.

13. Eva Brann, "The Spirit Lives in the Sticks," Stone, pp. 181–90.

14. George Anastaplo, "In re Allan Bloom: A Respectful Dissent," Stone, pp. 267–84.

15. Tom Hayden, "Our Finest Moment," Stone, pp. 344–49.

16. Charles Kesler, "*The Closing of the American Mind*: An Instant Classic Reconsidered," Stone, pp. 174–80.

17. Anastaplo, p. 281.

18. William R. Marty, "Athens and Jerusalem in *The Closing of the American Mind*," Stone, pp. 308–27.

19. William Galston, "Socratic Reason and Lockean Rights: The Place of the University in a Liberal Democracy," Stone, pp. 119–24.

20. Brann, p. 182.

5

The Problem of Democratic Individualism

From the vantage point of modern liberalism, and especially liberal democracy, America is not without its problems and limitations. The possibility even exists that America's apparently extreme partisanship on behalf of the individual could have the perverse effect of promoting the destruction of individuality or human distinctiveness. Alexis de Tocqueville named this American or democratic extremism individualism, and he claimed that it is the theoretical error that threatens the future of humanity.

The origin of individualism, or the idea of the solitary, self-sufficient human self, is still not well understood. It is accounted for with considerable persuasiveness in Tocqueville's *Democracy in America,* especially in its second volume, the one which has the democratic individual as its theme. But this book is almost never read well, especially by Americans.

Tocqueville's fear that its meaning would forever elude his readers remains well founded. It is difficult for us democrats to believe that Tocqueville really says that individualism is a democratic excess, and that its emergence, which is coincident with the progress of democracy, could be the cause of the abolition of humanity. We cannot help but believe that the cure for what ails democracy is more democracy. Even those American social scientists who attempt to follow in Tocqueville's footsteps are too dogmatically democratic, too American, one might say, to agree with or even really want to understand Tocqueville.

There is somewhat of a Tocqueville revival in America today. Its heart is perhaps the most widely acclaimed work in American social science in recent years, Robert Bellah et al.'s *Habits of the Heart.*[1] This book, an exploration of the limits of American individualism today, is a genuine and sometimes penetrating attempt to appropriate creatively Tocqueville's "new political science" for our time. It claims to be "explicitly and implicitly a detailed reading of, and commentary on, Tocqueville." Bellah could not, however, bring himself to agree with Tocqueville that the problem with America is too much democracy. Consequently, he explicitly dissents from Tocqueville's connection of the emergence of individualism with the progress of democracy or equality. For Bellah, individualism is the enemy of democracy, emerges in opposition to it, and can be eradicated by more of it. His immediate adversaries are Ronald Reagan and other allegedly anti-egalitarian, individualistic proponents of "neo-capitalism."

Actually, Bellah accepts much of Tocqueville's analysis. His precise position is this: to the extent the idea of the individual is democratic or egalitarian, it is salutary. To the extent it is undemocratic, it is pernicious, or individualism in Tocqueville's sense. The goodness of democracy or egalitarianism is his first principle. His dogmatism on this point is what, above all else, separates him from Tocqueville. My purpose is to examine both Tocqueville and Bellah to illuminate the problem of democratic individualism.

Tocqueville argues, and Bellah agrees, that democratization dissolves the ties or duties which link human beings to one another—those that constitute the family, religion, and political community. Each of them is to some extent inegalitarian or undemocratic. They, for the democrat, require the illegitimate subordination of the individual to other human beings. Democratization means freeing the individual from the rule of others for self-rule. Bellah sees this movement as destroying inequalities through "the absolute commitment to individual dignity." On the basis of his affirmation of its success, he asserts that today it is "intolerable" to compel the individual to defer uncritically to the authority of others. He or she should be free to live however he or she thinks best. All assertions of the existence of a common moral authority in matters of personal morality, for example, in matters concerning sex and family, are manifestations of "authoritarianism."

The problem with this destruction of authority, both Tocqueville and Bellah agree, is that the complete self-sufficiency or autonomy required by radical individualism is impossible for human beings. For Tocqueville, radical individualism and radical egalitarianism really point to the same thing—atomism. Atomism is the result of the destruction of all that binds human beings to one another and all that distinguishes them from one another.

An atomistic world would be one full of a mass of equally insignificant, identical, isolated selves, each of which is radically free from all external duties and restraints that might determine the purpose and direction of its existence. This freedom is freedom for an impossible task:

the human self cannot originate its own content out of nothing. The atoms are alike because they are equally without distinctively human content.

The very perception of unlimited freedom by a human being is dizzying and terrifying. It is something from which the apparently radically liberated self desires above all to escape. Without communal resources to shape and limit self-determination, the democratic self chooses not to determine itself, not to exercise its freedom. It passively defers to public opinion, Tocqueville says.[2] But this opinion itself is determined by no self in particular. The democratic self really seems to defer to some principle of impersonal materialism. It has no point of view from which to differentiate itself from its "environment." Radical individualism makes individual distinctiveness—individuality in any meaningful sense—impossible.

Both Tocqueville and Bellah call attention to the unendurable misery of this unsupported self—the one which is free from the undemocratic or anti-individualistic illusions which once bound human beings to religion, family, and political community. The liberated self is not full of the self-confidence that might make genuine autonomy possible. It is all too aware that it is not a god. It is aware primarily of its radical contingency or neediness. It knows that it cannot really satisfy its own deepest longings. The deepest of these, according to Tocqueville (but not Bellah), is the longing for immortality. Yet the deepest consequence of the perception of the truth of individualism is that one has no choice but to attempt to satisfy one's desires all by oneself.

Bellah follows Tocqueville both through his examination of affluent Americans and in his observation that the democratic individual is restless even in the midst of abundance. No amount of material success can wholly satisfy human desires, those which are at the root of the need for morality and religion. Democratic individuals continue to pursue even greater amounts of such success only because they believe they have no choice but to hope that somehow it can become satisfying. No other standard of success is credible to them. Because their hope is unreasonable, and Bellah never tires of pointing out the incoherence of American arguments based upon it, democratic individuals tend to avoid the leisure that might lead to self-contemplation. Their need to work hard has remarkably little to do with want in the usual sense. But it seems they cannot work hard enough.

In a self-consciously individualistic time, they can hardly hope to avoid self-contemplation altogether.

Bellah and Tocqueville agree that democratic individuals cannot help but be anxious, sometimes even melancholic. They are susceptible to religious madness and ideological fanaticism on the one hand and the pantheistic lullabies of therapists on the other. Generally speaking, their reason tends to give way. If their humanity is sustained, it is only through an assertion of will. This self-destruction of the mind occurs most readily among the most talented democratic individuals, the ones who are most aware of the futility of democratic striving but who see no credible alternative to it.[3]

For Bellah and Tocqueville, a related problem with democratic individualism, the one which makes it not really democratic, according to Bellah, is that its destruction of qualitative or community-generating human distinctions causes economic distinctiveness to become far too important. The result is a materialistic assertiveness or competitiveness which distorts all of human life. The idea that individuality is rooted only in materialism really produces nothing but misery. It produces poverty and related forms of human degradation for those who fail in the race of life. It also produces the anxiety of extreme self-consciousness for those who succeed. Both the affluent and the impoverished have reason to be radically dissatisfied with a wholly democratic individualism. In America's mostly middle class, democratic society, it is the dissatisfaction of the affluent that is politically significant. It is their opinions that Bellah criticizes. He wants to heighten their anxiety and lead them to acknowledge the cause of their misery.

For Bellah, the cure for the misery of individualism is the completion of democracy or "economic democracy." It is his contention that the misery and anxiety of democratic affluence would disappear in the process of the democratic destruction of economic distinctions. He is somewhat unclear concerning why this would occur. He has the propensity to equate anxiety with guilt. Affluent individuals know they do not deserve the affluence that sets them apart from other human beings. They are worried about being able to sustain it in economic competition. They know it causes undeserved suffering by others; they are afraid of these others. Their "hearts" or "consciences" call them to participate in the creation of genuinely egalitarian communities, to commit themselves to alleviating the suffering of the economically oppressed. Such commitment brings affluent individuals' own anxiety to an end. They are no longer isolated by their wealth and competitiveness.

Once one looks beyond Bellah's rhetorical cleverness and method-ological pretense, it becomes clear that he writes as a partisan of socialism. He suggests that America's most successful socialist, Eugene Debs, was the paradigmatic appropriator of the American tradition for this century. He also, following the lead of other contemporary American socialist intellectuals, makes the case for understanding American populism as indigenous socialism. Even in light of Bellah's argument, however, one cannot help but observe that socialism has never been popular in America, and most Americans still believe it to be antagonistic to their tradition. Bellah responds to this observation by criticizing the opinions of most Americans. He takes his bearings from what he believes a consistent articulation of the American tradition to be. He tries to improve America through using the Socratic method in the service of egalitarianism.

Bellah's opinion that socialism is the appropriate culmination of the American tradition as the only antidote to its self-destructive individualism is the product of logical deduction. He calls it the deepest insight of the biblical and republican—or to some extent anti-individualistic—elements of the American tradition. It is the only one of these insights, apparently, which has not been rendered incredible by the progress of democracy or individualism. Socialism is, in principle, the only regime more democratic than democratic individualism; it is more consistently egalitarian.

It is also correct to call Bellah a Marxist, although, in doing so, I do not want to be misunderstood. He was not a partisan of the Soviet Union. He is, more generally, a sincere opponent of totalitarianism. He believes he is interpreting the development of the American tradition correctly. He is right to imply that the Tocquevillian and the Marxian analyses of the excesses of individualism are similar, and he is to be applauded for discovering that Tocqueville thought through more clearly than Marx many of the key Marxian insights. By calling Bellah a Marxist I only mean to say that he leans toward the Marxian, rather than the Tocquevillian, solution to the problem of democratic individualism.

Tocqueville and Marx seem to agree that radical individualism is unendurable for human beings. Tocqueville contends that it must be moderated by religion and other "aristocratic" or qualitatively-based ideas for the idea of the individual or human distinctiveness to endure. If religion—or the truth of the idea of the soul—cannot be sustained in democratic times, then socialism is not only inevitable but perhaps even beneficial.

Tocqueville believed that the perpetuation of religion in democratic times was possible because the human soul really exists. Human beings have nonmaterialistic or spiritual needs which must be satisfied wherever they exist. The end of religion would signal the end of humanity, and Tocqueville did not think that the destruction of humanity is necessarily the final consequence of the unalterable progress of democracy.

Bellah wants to do justice to both religion and socialism, but he cannot do the impossible. Socialism is really his choice. His propensity is to reduce religion to the theology of liberation, to an instrument for bringing socialism into being. He praises the perspective of today's "mainstream" Protestant intellectual establishment, the one which identifies religion almost wholly with the cause of socialism. He also contends that Catholicism finally came into its own after Vatican II, by which he seems to mean that its leaders lost interest in almost everything but economic reform and opposing nuclear war.

Bellah shares Marx's enthusiasm for the possibility that the destruction of economic individualism, as the only form of inequality left in the world, would be the definitive triumph of democracy. Tocqueville fears that democracy's victory would be humanity's defeat. While Tocqueville is willing to be a partisan of war, although, of course, not all wars, Bellah and Marx affirm doctrines which point to a world without war, because it would be without individual competitiveness.

Would an egalitarian redistribution of wealth be sufficient to create such a world? Only if human discontents and the aggressiveness they produce have fundamentally an economic cause. But why are Tocqueville's and Bellah's Americans restless in the midst of abundance? They are pained by their consciousness of their individuality, their self-consciousness. They are anxious not about the scarcity of economic resources but about the scarcity of time. They know far too well that the pleasures of life are fleeting. They do not have time enough to enjoy. Their happiness is undermined by the intensity of their consciousness of time.

Their human misery comes from the fact that for them being human is little more than that consciousness. Only through the destruction of self-consciousness, which is always part of human existence, could the human discontents which produce war, competitiveness, and aggressiveness disappear. Do Bellah and Marx share the hope that the excesses of individualism will destroy human individuality or self-consciousness altogether? If so, that is the reason they do not share Tocqueville's moderation. Tocqueville opposes the excesses of individualism on behalf of the human individual.

Consider what a Tocquevillian account of the most powerful reason for the attractiveness of Marxism for democratic intellectuals would be. For the Marxist, in truth, the lesson of the experience of unadorned or wholly democratic individualism is that humanity itself is worthless. The resulting hatred of the human condition produces the final revolution, the one against all human distinctions or self-consciousness. This revolution is for the reintegration of human existence into non-human nature, for the wholly "species being." It is for the end of human freedom. It, to be sure, is also in the service of egalitarian consistency. The idea of human freedom cannot sustain itself indefinitely in light of the skeptical materialism that has fueled the democratic or egalitarian movement in thought.

There is something unfair about the identification of Bellah or even Marx with this conclusion. Both individuals really believe that a comprehensively egalitarian reconstitution of society could produce an unparalleled manifestation of human freedom. Bellah, for example, hopes for the replacement of the merely extrinsic satisfactions of economic reward with the intrinsic rewards of worthwhile work well-done. Only with the destruction of the former, he believes, could the latter come into its own. He also notes that materialistic restlessness of democratic individualism distracts the individual from contemplation of the "mystery of being" in communion with fellow human beings. There are other classical and biblical elements in Bellah's criticism of democratic individualism. His opposition to this individualism, like Tocqueville's, is partly from the perspective of an individual with an aristocratic attachment to intellectual excellence, to the idea that the truly human pursuits must be understood as choiceworthy for their own sakes.

Bellah revolts against democratic individualism partly because souls like his are not properly appreciated by the mixture of oligarchy and democracy which largely characterizes today's American regime. He is surely extremely aristocratic in his attachment to a vision of a world full of human excellence undistorted by materialistic competition. He has a far more difficult time coming to terms with democracy as it really exists among human beings than Tocqueville did.

Bellah is a Marxist, ultimately, because he shares with Marx the hope that the radicalization of the democratic principle can somehow satisfy his aristocratic longings, those of his soul. His remark concerning the common contemplation of the mystery of being is not a characteristic one. He opposes, for the most part, the "depolitization" of religion. His enthusiasm for the radical possibilities of egalitarian thought leads him, for the most part, to reduce morality to political morality and the Bible to a call for economic justice and pacifism. Perhaps this enthusiasm is evidence for the assertion that the attractiveness of Marxism for human beings, and especially democratic intellectuals, is in its assertion that the misery of human individuality was created by and hence can be destroyed by human beings. We can deliver ourselves from our self-created misery through the further making of history.

Tocqueville denies that history could ever provide a solution to the problem of human misery. As a result, he cannot share Bellah's enthusiasm for socialism. It is a democratic excess, a radical revolution against the truth about the human condition. According to Tocqueville: "The short space of three score years can never content the imagination of man; nor can the imperfect joys of the world satisfy his heart." These "joys," we must emphasize, include the participation in and even the achievement of radical social reform.

Tocqueville goes on: "Man alone, of all created beings, displays a natural contempt for existence, and yet a boundless desire to exist; he scorns life, but he dreads annihilation."[4] The contradictions expressed here—those, as Tocqueville puts it, of the beast with the angel in him—are the deepest source of human misery.[5] According to Marx, religion will disappear when human misery does. That might well be true. But the misery to which Tocqueville calls attention cannot be eradicated through social reform, unless such reform can somehow or another bring humanity to an end. Because Tocqueville is a partisan of human freedom, even at the expense of happiness or contentment, he could not recommend such reform. Its goal, no doubt, would be the divinization of humanity. But, because such a goal cannot be reached through merely human effort, its result would be humanity's brutalization.

Tocqueville traces the beginning of the democratic or egalitarian movement in thought to the sixteenth or seventeenth century. It is based on the skeptical denial that the human being has a soul or spiritual needs and a spiritual being. The bias of democratic thought against religion, one which Tocqueville observed when he called the religion of Americans their most precious aristocratic inheritance, is really a bias against the human condition or human individuality as it really exists. The self-sufficient or isolated and autonomous individual it apparently promotes is not human.

Bellah sometimes rightly criticizes the opinions of Americans with this conclusion in mind, but he fails to show how his radicalization of the egalitarian principle restores the idea of the human individual or human dignity. Socialism as a comprehensive, constitutive principle of society is radical democracy. It is also, according to Tocqueville, the enemy of the individual and of religion.

According to Tocqueville, Americans will remain partisans of human liberty as long as they remain religious, and they remain remarkably religious even today. They have not and must not abandon the idea of God, which subordinates human beings, even if all human beings equally, to Itself and hence limits self-rule in the name of egalitarian principle. Such consistency would not only be without God but without human individuality. Human beings, to remain human, must come to terms with their human desires and human suffering. They must prefer their human freedom to mindless, servile contentment. Tocqueville did not think that they could do so if they did not believe religion was in some sense or another true, if they did not believe in God or the soul.

In our time, no one has understood the genuinely radical truth that the fundamental human choice is between the truth of religion and the truth of socialism better than Aleksandr Solzhenitsyn. According to him, the essence of socialist ideology is the assertion that the value of the individual depends upon the success of social reform. It deprives individuals of any point of view from which to differentiate themselves from society. They are reduced to a social product and nothing more; they "democratically" lose their individuality.

Religion, or at least biblical religion, sees individuals as creatures of God. As creatures made in God's image, they possess a freedom that is given to them, not by society, but by God. They are free to acknowledge in their hearts their subordination to the will of God. Religious belief gives individuals a point of view or "inner" freedom to resist the lie of socialist ideology and maintain their genuinely individual dignity.

It goes without saying that Tocqueville would not have agreed with all of Solzhenitsyn's political analysis. But on the analysis of the problem of democratic individualism he is much closer to him than to Bellah. Democratic individualism or materialism cannot, by itself, sustain human liberty.

NOTES

1. Robert Bellah, Richard Madsen, William M. Sullivan, Ann Swidler, and Steven M. Tipton, *Habits of the Heart* (Berkeley: University of California Press, 1985). Since this essay was written, these authors published *The Good Society* (New York: Knopf, 1991), which makes explicit many of the policy implications of the analysis in *Habits*. The continuity of Bellah's concerns in his various books is shown nicely by Bruce Frohnen, "Robert Bellah and the Politics of 'Civil Religion'," *The Political Science Reviewer* 22 (Spring 1992), pp. 148–218.

2. Alexis de Tocqueville, *Democracy in America*, trans. G. Lawrence (New York: Harper and Row, 1988), pp. 434–36.

3. See *ibid.*, especially pp. 534–38.

4. *Ibid.*, pp. 296–97. The view of Tocqueville found throughout this essay is defended in my *The Restless Mind: Alexis de Tocqueville on the Origin and Perpetuation of Human Liberty* (Savage, MD: Rowman and Littlefield, 1993).

5. See *ibid.*, pp. 546–47. As I explain in *The Restless Mind*, Tocqueville's understanding of the human condition is also Pascal's. See, for example, the very Pascalian account in *Democracy*, p. 487.

6

How Education Became Illiberal

Dinesh D'Souza's justly acclaimed best seller *Illiberal Education* (Free Press, 1991) is a classic example of muckraking journalism. Muckraking is an inevitable and often salutary feature of writers in a liberal democracy. In a society such as ours, citizens tend to believe that the claims of democracy—the opinions and tastes of the majority—ought to be limited by liberty. But this consent to liberty is given in the trust that it be used for its proper purposes. The muckraker exposes abuses of that trust, corruption in respected institutions.

The original muckrakers exposed the irresponsible use of economic liberty. D'Souza exposes flagrant and often bizarre misuses of intellectual liberty. Economic corruption is easy to account for as what happens when human selfishness is not properly checked. The intellectual disorder is much harder to explain, and D'Souza does not even claim to have done an adequate job of doing so.

The danger of muckraking is that the majority is often too easily aroused. Anger can produce extreme and illiberal responses to abuses which are merely abuses. When it comes to intellectual liberty, the possibility is particularly strong that the majority can be provoked to confuse its proper use with its abuse. People often think that what professors do when lost in thought is strange and useless, but it is not always. One of the most hardy thoughts of Socrates is that the philosopher will always seem insane to citizens.

D'Souza actually seems to want to avoid this illiberal danger. He writes not against higher education, but on its behalf. He shows that our best universities have abandoned their devotion to liberal education. Professors no longer believe that education is the way to wisdom, to freedom from convention, accident, and circumstance. They still demand intellectual freedom, but they cannot explain why. They still speak of freedom from political control as a right, but they teach that no one is really free from that control. If the pretensions of liberal education are an illusion, then the people ought to withdraw their consent to the university's liberty.

D'Souza points to this illiberal conclusion in order decisively to reject it. He appeals to the prejudice Americans have in favor of intellectual liberty. He suggests that the unsophisticated many have a sounder view of that liberty than the erudite few. The ruling group—the majority—believes that there are genuine limitations on the ruling group's power, whereas our professors characteristically do not.

The university's freedom depends upon the Socratic opinion that truth is more fundamental than and sets limits on political power. The fact that this opinion is shared by the majority in America depends upon the perception that it is both Socratic and biblical, in accord with both reason and revelation. The Bible and Socrates agree that the truth shall set us free, and hence those who are especially devoted to its pursuit should be especially free.

Our professors have deconstructed or discredited the authority of both Socrates and the Bible. They have shown that they have no right—except the unlimited right to defraud—to be free. Because they rule within their sphere illegitimately or without right, it is only a matter of time before they are exposed and overthrown. D'Souza arouses us on behalf of liberal education in order that we not be aroused later against all of higher education.

But our righteous anger directed against professorial tyranny and even on behalf of liberal education should not blind us to the fact that America's devotion to that education has never been unreserved or unambiguous. It may also be the case that the majority, or at least a relatively unsophisticated and religious elite, has always been more attached to liberal education than the most sophisticated or enlightened of our intellectual leaders. The deconstruction of liberal education had already begun with our leading Founders. Today's politically correct professors claim, with some justice, merely to have worked through certain of their most innovative thoughts.

The Founders and Liberal Education
Our Founders, to be sure, were rationalists. They held, in Jefferson's stirring phrase, that "the light of science" could free us from all forms of tyranny. They defended intellectual liberty as a natural right against both religious and political authority. They distinguished clearly between truth and majority opinion. They taught that the same universal principles

should inform societies or political communities everywhere and at all times.

The Founders, however, did not simply affirm the Socratic and biblical tradition of liberal education. They thought the Socratic view of higher education as a leisurely inquiry in pursuit of answers to fundamental human questions was theoretically wrongheaded and practically oppressive. Jefferson, for example, wrote that the contemplative rationalism of the ancient philosophers produced, in him, the personal serenity that leads to happiness. But he also viewed those philosophers as selfish and elitist. The happiness or pleasure they promoted is available to a gifted and fortunate few, and it did not support the duties of those few—the philosophers—to the non-philosophers.

The source of morality, for Jefferson, was not the "Great Books" education he enjoyed and D'Souza promotes. It was in a natural inclination or instinct he called the "moral sense," which could only be distorted by reflection. Such reflection he called "Platonizing" moralism, a sort of moral tyranny rooted in ridiculous mystifications.

For Jefferson, democratic education was, in part, a revolt against the Platonic-Christian moralizing he found in much of the tradition of liberal education on behalf of the simple, natural inclination of democratic benevolence. This benevolence was an indispensable support to the modern or Enlightenment theoretical conclusion, which Jefferson also accepted, that education should be mainly useful or productive. It should transform the world through the application of science to the solution of human problems with the security and comfort of all human beings in mind.

With this conclusion in mind, Jefferson conspired to eliminate classical and Christian morality as viable alternatives in America. He undertook the project of censoring the Bible, removing all doctrine that struck him as unreasonable, that depended on Platonism or revelation. Because his project was a partial failure, most Americans remained more attached to traditional morality than he thought best. Still, Jefferson's project, informed as it was by a certain "political correctness," did succeed in narrowing the scope of opinion in America. D'Souza notes, for example, that he finds much less genuine diversity of opinion in America than in his native India.

Pragmatism

Jefferson's views that education should be unleisurely or useful, rooted in a democratic morality, and informed by the anti-traditional "light of science" are the foundations of American pragmatism. John Dewey was doubtlessly the most influential and most astute of the theorists called pragmatists, but there is not much particularly remarkable or innovative in Dewey's writing. Pragmatism—or the identification of the good, true, and beautiful with the useful, and hence of art and science or all of education with technology—Alexis de Tocqueville had already identified as the opinion which informs enlightened or liberal democracy as such. It combines the liberal devotion to intellectual freedom or scientific liberation with the materialistic tastes and opinions of a skeptical or individualistic majority. What is missing in pragmatism that is present in Jefferson's thought is the identification of personal serenity and happiness with contemplation. But Jefferson knew that insofar as he was an ancient philosopher he was undemocratic and unpragmatic.

Pragmatism democratizes education, above all, by avoiding questions that do not arise immediately from the problems of daily life. It is, as Tocqueville observed, positively hostile to the human spirit rising above those concerns, which it will do if it is not held down. Hence it is hostile to the leisurely concerns of liberal education, to genuinely radical reflection about the human condition.

What pragmatism attempts to suppress, as Tocqueville, again, first noticed, is the miserable anxiety experienced by the self-conscious mortal, the one who discovers that her condition cannot really be transformed by the progress of democracy and science. Tocqueville explains that pragmatism is most opposed to the spirit of Pascal. His psychologically penetrating inquiry into the human meaning of modern science reveals a truth that human beings must avoid to live well. Dewey, despite his many elegant accounts of change, uncertainty, and growth and decay in the human experience, never discusses the experience of the individual's awareness of the fact that he will die alone.

Pragmatism preserves the devotion to reason or science that justifies the university's liberty. But it dogmatically dismisses unproductive human inquiry. It does so, officially, on the premise that such inquiry is undemocratic and wasteful. But pragmatists seems, more fundamentally, to know that its most powerful effect, contrary to Jefferson's personal experience, is to make human beings miserably anxious about their arbitrary and contingent existence in an infinite universe.

Tocqueville, following the first great critic of Enlightenment, Rousseau, and the Christian psychologist, Pascal, says that scientific and democratic progress have made human beings more powerful, prosperous, and free, but also more restless, discontent, anxious, and easily disappointed. Happiness or contentment, which human beings enjoyed more readily in feudal times despite or because of their poverty, oppression, and ignorance, have been replaced by the pursuit of happiness, which has turned out to be the right to be incessantly restless and to defer enjoyment indefinitely. Tocqueville presents the enlightened, calculating Americans as succumbing, with growing frequency, to melancholy and madness, because they have found their unprecedented liberty unendurable. The pragmatic understanding of liberty produces mental self-destruction.

The pragmatic view of science has the effect of destroying the illusions and beliefs that sustain human liberty. The practical efforts of human beings to make their existences less precarious or contingent have the perverse effect of making them more so. The progress of science and democracy does not, as the Enlightenment philosophers promised, liberate human beings from the misery of their condition, but rather intensifies it. The progress is toward the universalization of Pascal's experience of fearful, anxious loneliness in a universe which provides no support for one's particular existence. Pragmatism cannot help but be replaced by existentialism.

As human beings come to perceive themselves more clearly as miserable accidents, they come to think of themselves as deserving of nothing but compassion. They are miserable through no fault of their own, and there is nothing to be done about it. This compassion discredits the goodness of intellectual liberty, which turns out to be for nothing but the experience of oneself as absolutely contingent.

Pragmatism, in short, readily deconstructs itself. It is replaced by a compassionate revelation of the truth about the human condition, which it attempted to suppress but could not. We are all victims, living in a highly self-conscious and disbelieving and hence miserable time. If education has any function, it is to free us from what remains of the illusion that we can free ourselves from our victim status. Its purpose is to give us, first of all, compassion for ourselves.

Post-Pragmatist Education

What D'Souza describes is post-pragmatist education. It seems to be madness from the traditional perspective of liberal education. But it is, in its way, more coherent than pragmatism's incomplete rejection of that tradition. What D'Souza describes is education reduced to victimology.

All human thought, today's deconstructionist professor asserts, is determined by ones's race and gender, and perhaps sexual orientation and class. We did not choose these characteristics, and we cannot transcend them. We are determined by the accidental features of our condition. If we are white and male, we cannot help but oppress. If we are "minority" and female, we cannot help but be oppressed.

White male oppressors are morally or politically correct to the extent they are sensitive, which means, to begin with, feeling compassion for the unfortunate plight of minorities. This plight, of course, is caused by the oppressors, but only accidentally. They cannot even take pride in their conquests.

Oppressors are sensitized to the truth that whatever separates them from the oppressed is accidental, because everything which is distinctively human is accidental. They have no right to take pride in their distinctiveness or view it as their right. They also have no right to feel anger when it is taken away by an arbitrary or capricious public policy. Affirmative action so understood becomes an educational method. It shows the oppressors that they are also dependent upon forces beyond their control. What they believed to be their own is not theirs at all. The truth of affirmative action is not grasped simply by feeling compassion for minorities, but by feeling it for oneself.

The oppressors have the moral imperative to become hypersensitive, purging themselves of all anger. But the oppressed, as D'Souza reports, are encouraged not to restrain their anger at all. They are to use it to suppress the sensitivity they might otherwise feel for their oppressors as equally unfree, equally determined by their race, gender, or class.

This moral inegalitarianism—the requirement of inhuman self-restraint from some and inhuman assertiveness from others—seems to be in the service of ultimate equality. The masters are to act like slaves, and the slaves like masters, in the hope that all will become alike. But how this is to happen is deceptively complex. The anger of the oppressed really opposes their genuine assertiveness, the desire they might otherwise have genuinely to improve their own condition, to become masters of their own fate.

The anger of the oppressed is beyond criticism in order to ensure its extremism. D'Souza suggests the comparison of the anger of aroused African American and Asian American students. The latter, of course, is not officially recognized as minority anger, and it really is not. The anger of the Asian Americans is moderate. It is based on the premise that their condition, presently sometimes quite unfortunate, can be improved decisively through their hard work. Anger is moderated by hope, and hope generates effective self-assertion.

Asian American anger is also moderated by the perception of the justice of the American principle of "equality of opportunity," which gives them a chance to succeed on American terms. Their anger becomes only somewhat less moderate in the face of the injustice of affirmative action. So far, it is only a distortion and not a wholesale destruction of the American principle. There is still hope, because there is still some opportunity.

Because Asian Americans do not yet understand how unfortunate the human condition, including their own condition, really is, they seem to flourish in America. They do so, however, only because America is not yet compassionate or sensitive enough. Asian Americans still have much to learn.

D'Souza quotes an Asian American student who recently escaped from Vietnam on a boat to the effect that she is lucky to have suffered less than American blacks. She knows that blacks have suffered more because their anger is so much greater. What the African American knows that the Asian American does not is that he or she will always suffer from oppression. His or her anger is a product of hopelessness, which is sensitively recognized but not really alleviated by affirmative action. Affirmative action is no longer understood as simply a correction or perfection of equality of opportunity, as a policy required to give minorities a genuine chance to succeed. Such an understanding is insufficiently compassionate or sensitive.

It turns out that the extreme anger of minorities is a manifestation of their extreme sensitivity to their own plight. It opposes efforts at personal improvement as inevitably futile. White hypersensitivity and minority anger have the same educational goal: to put one in the mood that best reflects the truth about the human condition, and hence denies the possibility of human success.

Ableism and Human Dignity

This conclusion is clear in the most striking "ism," or "specific manifestation of oppression," found in a document prepared by the Smith College Office of Student Affairs for the freshmen of Fall 1990. This document was instantly notorious and has been widely quoted for its extremism, and hence its instructiveness. It defines "ableism" as "oppression of the differently abled, by the temporarily able."

Ableism might be understood in a way that is rather uncontroversial. It might refer to the oppression of those who used to be called handicapped based upon the opinion that the handicap reflects something more fundamental about a person's condition than it really does. Everyone—politically correct and incorrect—can see that such pretentiousness depends upon a lack of compassion, on an inability to perceive the role of fortune in human affairs and the ways in which all human beings are essentially equal. But the extremely politically correct definition denies that there is such a thing as ability at all. Compassion, instead of merely revealing something about the human condition, obliterates everything else.

The abled are only "temporarily abled." Their abilities are useless because they cannot conquer time. In the end, we are all disabled by our contingency and mortality. "Ableism" means not recognizing that in the light of that fact all human distinctions are meaningless. It means insensitivity to the fact that we are all disabled by our condition.

It would seem that this perception that we are all equally disabled cannot be reconciled with the emphasis on dignity or respect that is also part of post-pragmatist political correctness. D'Souza describes an impressive number of efforts to censor language that would, even unwittingly, insult or degrade minorities. Dignity is more fundamental than freedom to speak one's mind.

This dignity is new because it is sensitive or compassionate. All human beings are equally worthless. Nothing they are or can accomplish can really be respected. Hence dignity must be based on a decision to ignore the truth. We simply grant dignity to one another. It is a kind of solace, although a rather ineffective one. Its source of value is too obviously arbitrary.

Because dignity is threatened by the truth, in its name we must suppress the truth. It goes without saying that this suppression depends upon knowledge of the truth. One must know that it will make one miserable in order to oppose it. This ineffective effort at thought control is an extreme version of a propensity that already existed under pragmatism.

Compassionate Relativism

D'Souza finds the most extreme suppression of the truth in politically correct evaluations of non-Western cultures. They are also not to be criticized, although they are characteristically full of inegalitarianism, sexism, and conspicuously lacking in compassion. The relativism that makes them beyond criticism is the product of the Western or radically enlightened opinion that all human distinctions are equal in dignity and equally worthless. But non-Western societies never accept that opinion. Relativism seems to make it impossible to criticize non-relativistic opinion, whereas non-relativists, with their assertiveness, cannot help but criticize relativism.

It seems that the non-relativists have all the advantages. But the politically correct view is still to view non-Western cultures as victims of Western oppression. Although politically correct professors rarely defend this view correctly, it does make sense from the perspective of compassionate relativism. What the West has done has been to destroy the credibility of non-Western societies by relativizing their values. Their citizens have become progressively more Western. In many cases, they, as a result, have become more wealthy, powerful, and free. But in the decisive sense, they have also become more restless and miserable. They, too, have come to see themselves as nothing but accidents.

What the West gives to the rest of the world by universalizing and homogenizing it is human misery. It destroys the beliefs and illusions that protected human life from the truth. Compassionate relativism suggests that non-Western cultures are always superior in the sense that the people who live under their domination are more happy or content, or less deserving of compassion.

D'Souza does well in showing that the politically correct investigation of non-Western cultures is hardly ever serious scholarship. There is no genuine attempt to enter the "spirit" of their worlds. That would take decades of study and enormous self-discipline. The study begins with the premise that it is impossible to capture that spirit, because it is already dead.

A compassionate relativist cannot really experience what it is like not to be one, and he or she believes that everyone is on the way to becoming one. But the idea that human beings have not always been miserable, which can be grasped through a superficial consideration of what it means to be non-Western, heightens one's sensitivity to one's Western plight.

It is worth emphasizing that such study of non-Western cultures must be condescending and dogmatic. It begins with the chauvinistic premise that they are less enlightened than we are, and that their lack of enlightenment is the cause of their contentment. It is the chauvinism of Rousseau's *Discourse on Inequality*, which seems to equate non-Western with less human. This chauvinism, of course, is also at the foundation of Marx's history, the lens through which non-Western societies are characteristically understood. Even the opinion that Western universalism has reduced human distinctiveness to worthlessness cannot really "deconstruct" its claim to superiority.

Negative Universalism

The core claim of this universalism—which begins with the emergence of philosophy among the Greeks and is forcefully present in our founding documents—is that what is most fundamental is what all human beings share in common, what is according to nature. This universal standard judges and finds wanting the merely conventional or particular assertions of human value by the various societies or cultures. This standard is "deconstructed" with the theoretical perception that human beings are never free from what is particular or accidental.

Universalism turns out to be true only negatively. It reveals the accidental to be merely accidental. But it is unable to replace it with what is universal. Hence the history of the West is the emptying of the world of value. The Socratic or biblical pursuit of universal truth is devastating for the existence of beings who come to know they are merely particular.

Before affirmative action, the American view was that race is accidental, or irrelevant to what is universal or "essential" about human nature. Racial differences, as a result, ought to be irrelevant in a society dedicated to protecting the natural rights of individuals, one which views all human beings as essentially beings with rights. Race (and sex and sexual orientation) become essential only when the difference between essence and accident disappears, when the accidental becomes the essential.

It might seem that compassion for the accidental or unfortunate character of the human condition would unite all human beings by overcoming the pretensions of individualism. But it has, more fundamentally, separated us. The accident of my whiteness keeps me from comprehending the accident of your blackness. The fact that blackness and whiteness are equally arbitrary does not, apparently, reduce one to the other.

Some way to articulate universal human experience seems to be necessary for me to share my misery with you. We, without it, are in the same boat, but still too separated to share our experience. We have none of the advantages of either universality or particularity, but the burdens of both.

We can now see what it really means to affirm the truth of "cultural diversity." If one lives in a vital culture, one lives certain of its superiority or at least its greatness. If one is a philosopher or a believer in biblical revelation, one lives in the light of the unity beyond the diversity. Diversity remains a fact, but not the most fundamental one. If one sees culture as fundamental and merely arbitrary and hence irreducibly diverse, one lives outside of culture but without philosophy or God, with the most miserable of truths. It is no wonder that the perception of "cultural diversity" produces bizarre doctrines and censorship. It might be only a matter of time before there are far stronger reactions against the promulgation of its truth than we have seen so far.

Our politically correct professors cannot be blamed for not teaching what they believe to be true. We can blame them for believing that we are all equally unfree, and still demanding their freedom. Perhaps we can also blame them for teaching a truth that makes human life miserable by emptying human distinctions of their value. They reply, of course, that they do not really deconstruct, but merely report the results of history's deconstruction.

The Possibility of Liberal Education

Our professors, unlike D'Souza and perhaps most Americans, do not believe that liberal education is possible. If it is possible, it must be shown that the human condition is not merely accidental or arbitrary. The restoration of the possibility of liberal education requires liberal education. It requires the recovery of our faith in reason and revelation through the study of the "Great Books," because they contain the best arguments on their behalf.

To most of our most influential professors, such an attempt at recovery is reactionary. It is the project of those who are not yet truly educated or enlightened, who are not yet sensitive or compassionate enough. The fight for liberal education will require much more than showing the strange consequences of contemporary theory, its opposition to common sense and traditional American principle. That theory is too much the product of certain features of American thought from the beginning. It must be challenged on the level of theory. But D'Souza's muckraking is still salutary because those professors who must lead the fight are weak enough within the university to have no choice but to ally themselves with the people against their colleagues.

The political battle should be on behalf of genuine diversity. The principle of diversity within the university, as D'Souza notes, no longer includes those who hold opinions which are both Western and politically incorrect. It does not include those who hold that intellectual liberty is the greatest good for human beings, because it produces most intensely not misery and anxiety but pleasure and wisdom. Excluded is the opinion of Socrates and Jefferson.

Also excluded are "creationists," those who hold that human beings are not accidents but creatures of a personal God. They believe, with James Madison, that intellectual liberty is for discovering the duties of the creature to the Creator. They also believe that human misery and anxiety can and must be moderated by faith, which can be the foundation of our articulation of our common experiences.

These opinions, the politically correct believe, must be excluded because they are manifestly untrue. But the majority in this liberal democracy is not yet so convinced. Its help is indispensable for the relatively few professors who also hold that their truth can be defended.

One of those professors is Harvard's Harvey Mansfield, Jr. He, dismissed as a "crazy extremist" by the politically correct, emerges as the hero of D'Souza's book. His resolute opposition to hypersensitivity, including affirmative action, on behalf of human liberty and dignity has caused him "to become something of a pariah on the Harvard campus." But his intellectual isolation has not made him miserable and anxious. He says he welcomes the freedom "from asphyxiating social pressures" and "to speak his mind." He manifests the combination of personal serenity and freedom from the opinion of the ruling group that is at least reminiscent of Socrates or Jefferson. Academic freedom, in some cases, still protects liberal education. There is still hope that its abuses can be corrected.

7

Fukuyama Versus the End of History

The revolution of 1989, which brought down most existing socialist regimes and discredited the idea of socialism, was arguably the last of the modern revolutions. It is open to at least two extreme or radical interpretations.

The first is radically modern. Socialism failed because it contained reactionary "idealism," which opposed the free development of modern liberty and prosperity. Its failure shows that human beings were already definitively satisfied with the "classless society" of the United States, imitated by the other "advanced" nations of the world. Socialism and the revolution against it were the last manifestations of human spiritedness, what produces human action or history, in the world. History or human liberty has now come to an end. Human beings will now come to live everywhere as docile members of a "welfare state," gradually surrendering the details of the humanity or human liberty they have already surrendered in principle. Eventually, even the state itself will wither away. This end of history, with its eradication of the disorder of human liberty, is the culmination of modern or systematic rationalism. This view, we shall see, is found in the thought of Alexandre Kojève, although it was anticipated by the musings of Alexis de Tocqueville about "soft despotism."

A second view of the revolution of 1989, in its way almost as radical, is that the end of the modern world may mean the inauguration of a postmodern world. This world will be a new birth of human liberty or plurality, a world free from the pretentious and misanthropic illusions of modern rationalism. This postmodern view is found in many places today. Most strikingly, it was the interpretation given to the revolution by the dissident opponents to socialism or communism in Central and Eastern Europe.

Fukuyama's book attempts to find a middle way between Kojève's misanthropic view of modern rationalism and the postmodern rejection of that rationalism on behalf of human liberty or dignity. He wishes to combine that rationalism with the concern for the perception or even revitalization of the conditions for human liberty. He searches for an account of the end of history that is full of human or free and dignified beings. He fails, although perhaps nobly. The position he wishes to defend is indefensible.

Fukuyama argues that the world-wide triumph of liberal democracy is the end of history. His book's main deficiency is that it does not really make clear what the end of history must necessarily be. Fukuyama shares this deficiency with Marx, who also said, quite incoherently, that at the end of history man will remain a social and so human being. Incoherence is not necessarily a criticism of a book about human beings. But Fukuyama almost claims that he is a wise man because he views history (and so human existence) as a coherent whole.

The most misleading incoherence of Fukuyama's book is his combination of a seemingly moderate defense of the human dignity and liberal democracy with comprehensive atheism. He seems to hold that human liberty can be perpetuated in the absence of the distinction between man and God. With this suggestion, he departs from the rigor of the comprehensive atheism of his mentor, Kojève, as well as from that of Friedrich Nietzsche, whom he regards as Kojève's most thoughtful antagonist. Kojève and Nietzsche agree that the death of God, or, as Fukuyama puts it, the banishing of religion from the West by liberalism,[1] signals the end of human liberty or distinctiveness.

One sign of Fukuyama's incoherence is that he interprets the revolution of 1989 in a way that is both radically modern and a celebration of human dignity. He says, in effect, that that revolution can be viewed as the completion of the atheistic project of the modern philosophers to transform the world in the service of their thought. Man now has no need for God, because the Kingdom of God has come to earth, and there man rules.

The dominant view, of course, is that the revolution of 1989 was not the final stage in the revelation of the truth of this theology of liberation. It discredited that theology, and reinvigorated other forms that retained the distinction between man and God. For the most eloquent and profound of the dissidents, Aleksandr Solzhenitsyn and Václav Havel, the collapse of socialist totalitarianism was part of the modern world revealing itself to itself as an error.[2] The error is that there could be a systematic or merely historical or social solution to the disorder or liberty that characterizes human existence. For the dissidents, human liberty is, in part, freedom from such determination.

Any solution to the human problem, for Solzhenitsyn and Havel, must be individual and spiritual. That thought is the foundation for the reconstitution of a world that supports the individual's development. This world depends upon the recovery of the key human distinctions between good and evil and man and God, as well as the human person's openness to eternity. These distinctions are the foundation of human responsibility, which can still be exercised in our time. From this dissident perspective Fukuyama's book seems misanthropic and reactionary.

Kojève never hid the misanthropy of his description of the end of history as the here and now. He sought to show that human liberty or distinctiveness no longer exists, and he affirmed their disappearance as according to reason and according to nature. For him, human liberty is an error that manifested itself in and was finally corrected by history.

According to Kojève, there is no difference worth considering between today's Western liberal democracies and the socialist societies that used to make up the Soviet Bloc. Both are forms of the universal and homogeneous state, or the end of history. They both recognize, in principle, the dignity or liberty of all human beings as citizens equally well, and they both, in principle, reduce all human beings to "automatons."[3] It would seem that the recognition of dignity is a momentary prelude to the end of human liberty and self-consciousness.

But Fukuyama distinguishes clearly between the freedom and dignity of liberal democracy and the systematic efforts to destroy it under socialist or communist totalitarianism. He quite strikingly voices his agreement with Havel's account of human dignity and communism's futile attempt to negate it. He disguises his disagreement with Havel by not showing that, for Havel, dignity is "living in the truth," which means in part living with the awareness that one is not most fundamentally a historical being. In Fukuyama's hands, Havel's account of dignity becomes merely an assertion of one's freedom from fear, although he also says that this assertion characteristically masks the truth about itself to itself.[4]

Havel draws a quite different lesson for the West from the human victory in his nation. His people's successful resistance against efforts at systemization ought to inspire the Western nations to resist the systematic tendencies that animate their own societies. Human beings act humanly, or in accord with their dignity and openness to the truth, precisely when they resist all efforts to bring history to an end.

For Havel and Solzhenitsyn, liberal democracy remains superior to socialism only because it is not simply animated by the modern pretensions that fill the thought that history can end. But, for Fukuyama, liberal democracy is superior to socialism because it is history's true end. He aims to improve upon Kojève and satisfy Havel by purging the argument for the end of history of its misanthropy. He even suggests, quite incoherently, that the end of history cannot be simply systematic, because to perpetuate itself over time it must make room for human irrationality or disorder. History can come to an end only if it does not come to an end.

Such subtle thinking, of course, is really equivocation. Fukuyama also attempts to do justice to the strongest argument, in his view, against history's end. It comes from Nietzsche, on behalf of human dignity. But Nietzsche's view, finally, is much closer to Kojève's than Havel's. Kojève and Nietzsche both agree with the radically modern perception that God is dead. He had been killed by the development of human self-consciousness over time or history. God disappears either because men have become gods or because they have become unhistorical or unfree and contented animals. Kojève says, in fact, they have become both. For Nietzsche, the alternatives, in the absence of God, are the "last man," who, if not simply an animal, is without dignity or spirit, and the "overman," who surpasses mere humanity in his radical or self-consciously divine creativity. Fukuyama's book describes a world without God yet full of free and dignified men.

But Fukuyama's description of a godless world of unprecedented freedom and dignity sometimes seems not to be his last word. He tacks on accounts of Nietzsche's view of the "last man" and Kojève's description of the return of man to simple animality. But these radical views, in Fukuyama's hands, are defanged and so remarkably uncompelling. He never even presents Kojève's simple argument for the conclusion that man must disappear at the end of history. If man is a historical being and nothing more, which he must be if he is to recognize his perfection in history's end, then his recognition of that end is also a recognition of his own disappearance.

What I miss most in Fukuyama's book is a clear, consistent articulation of the view that man is a historical being. He does not show why that view of man claims to be the only empirically verifiable atheism, or the only atheism properly so-called. So he makes it far too easy for us to believe what Kojève and Nietzsche (and Havel and Solzhenitsyn) do not, that human beings can live well in freedom and dignity without God.

The extent to which Fukuyama misuses Kojève in this way is sometimes astounding. He says, again most incoherently, that Kojève is wrong not to employ a teleological view of human nature to support his view that history has definitively satisfied human desire.[5] He makes it seem possible to use Socrates's tripartite account of human nature or the soul to judge the results of history.[6] At the end of history, the rational, spirited, and desiring parts of the soul are all satisfied. Science has conquered nature, producing the material plenty required to satisfy bodily desire. The spirited part of the soul is realistically or historically redefined as the desire for recognition, which is satisfied by the universal and homogeneous recognition of citizen by citizen in a world of liberal democracies. The rational part of the soul is satisfied by the fact that history has an order or system, and it is readily comprehensible at history's end. At the end of history, philosophy is replaced by wisdom, or complete knowledge or self-consciousness. What the wise man (Fukuyama) knows, in Fukuyama's eyes, is a complete account of the perfection of human nature. With this seemingly natural yet historically-won wisdom, Fukuyama can affirm history's success.

Fukuyama confuses us quite deliberately by presenting this teleological view in the text while leaving Kojève's empirical objection to it for the notes.[7] Human nature, in Kojève's eyes, is an oxymoron. The evidence is that what distinguishes man is his historical being, not his nature. His nature really is the same as that of other bodies in motion, obeying the same predictable, even mechanical, laws. Nature, so understood, has no *telos*, or at least no human end. If human beings have a purpose, it must be historical. It can only be known at the end of history, when their historical or distinctively human desire can be known to have received historical satisfaction.

Fukuyama's correction of Kojève about nature merely produces confusion. He relies on the authority of a letter of Leo Strauss to Kojève to support this correction.[8] The letter's point, as a whole, is that only a teleological conception of nature can keep man's existence or distinctiveness from seeming radically contingent. This observation is true. But it is hard to see how it is a criticism. The radical contingency of human existence is a necessary consequence of the radical distinction between nature and history. That distinction is required if one is to speak of the end of history.

The relationship between history and nature is contingent or accidental. Why man emerges in opposition to nature man cannot know. That history is inexplicable according to nature is a necessary premise of human freedom historically understood. That freedom must be complete freedom from all that is given by nature.

Strauss does say that, without a teleological conception of nature, Kojève cannot know whether the historical process he describes is unique. It may repeat itself here on earth or somewhere else. But Kojève cannot and does not deny that history might occur again. There is no reason why or why not. The accident might happen again. That fact has nothing to do with the rationality or circularity of Kojève's description of human freedom, and so of his satisfaction at history's end. Although history emerges accidentally against nature, it can still be shown to be an ordered or rational and human whole.

A human being is given a nature, as is every other animal, but he makes himself human. Human motion is actually a mixture of natural givenness and historical acquisition. But only the latter motion is distinctively human, or free from nature. With the disappearance of historical motion or action at the end of history, man once again becomes wholly determined, like every other animal, by nature.

Fukuyama reveals in a note that the identification of human with historical existence was first made not by Kojève or Hegel, but by Rousseau. He does not assess the significance of this fact or show the relationship between Rousseau's thought and Hegel's. In Rousseau's view, man, at the beginning or in the state of nature, was simply an animal.[9] Rousseau also anticipates that the end of history will be a return to man's beginning, to his wholly natural, asocial, and brutish existence.[10] The great merit of Kojève's wonderfully consistent Hegelianism is that he sees the necessity of this return clearly and without equivocation.

According to Rousseau, human beings begin as brutes, but with an inexplicable or accidental capacity for perfectibility or undetermined development away from nature. They make themselves more free in their attempts to satisfy their desires. But in the process they also create new desires which are more difficult to satisfy. History is, in part, human desires expanding more rapidly than the capacities to satisfy them.

As human beings become more free from nature, they become more self-conscious, or more aware of what they have made. Almost the first moment in the development of this self-consciousness is the awareness of one's mortality and so consciousness of time. Human beings become progressively more conscious of time, or self-conscious, over time. Human beings are historical and so temporal beings, the beings with time in them.

Historical development is in response to human discontent. Natural man is content; animals are content. Over time, man makes himself progressively more discontent in response to his discontent. He becomes more conscious of time, the consciousness which is the source of all distinctively human misery. That misery, in turn, is the source of all human disorder, including poverty, disease, inequality, hatred, vanity, and so forth. History, for Rousseau, is the record of human misery and disorder.

Human beings cannot be understood to have aimed to make themselves progressively more discontent. From the perspective of individual human beings, historical development must be understood as accidental. They move away from the health and contentment they were given by nature. From the perspective of nature, history is a misery-producing accident and nothing more.

So the lesson of history, according to nature, is that history is an error. Human beings ought to live according to nature, which means they ought to surrender what is distinctively human about their existence. Perfectly self-conscious mortals reject that consciousness. They may, at first, prefer their humanity or history in their pride. But they cannot help but see that all pride is vanity, because everything human is accidental. To be human, as we seem to see so clearly today, is to be a victim of one's place in history, to be deserving of compassion, not pride.

Where the Hegelians such as Kojève seem to differ from Rousseau is that they deny that human pride is vanity. The total independence of historical motion or action from the givenness of nature is proof of the existence of human freedom. At the end of history, human beings are perfectly conscious of their freedom. One knows that one's perception about one's own freedom is true, because it is recognized by other free beings. Human self-consciousness is necessarily social or reciprocal. So, paradoxically, the self-sufficiency of each, particular human can only be recognized in the social or political setting of the universal and homogeneous state, the end of all historical action. There, free citizens recognize one another's freedom, their dignity in being undetermined by nature.

But Kojève makes it clear that this reciprocal recognition of human freedom occurs only for a moment. Unlike Fukuyama, he does not worry about the conditions for its perpetuation, because he knows it is impossible. Human freedom is historical, or action in response to human desire. For Kojève, the only human or historical desire is for prideful consciousness of one's freedom from nature, or the desire for recognition. If that desire is satisfied, as it is in the universal and homogeneous state, then human beings will no longer act. They will no longer manifest or give evidence of their freedom in history. It is not human to be satisfied. The end of history must be the end of humanity.

Despite differences on details, Kojève shows that the Rousseauean and Hegelian conclusions are virtually indistinguishable. Man is a historical being. History is time. Man is the being with time in him. If he is historical, his existence is temporary. He comes into being and passes away in a cosmos indifferent to his existence. His disappearance, in retrospect, was inevitable and, as Kojève laconically says, no cosmic catastrophe. The species *homo sapiens* lives on in harmony with nature. What disappears is only the historical being, man properly so-called. The end of history, is, if anything, good for nature. The disorder of historical or human existence, as the ecologists say, mixes with, corrupts, and so threatens almost all natural order.[11]

Man disappears when he recognizes his total independence or freedom from nature. He realizes his self-consciousness is "nothing," or merely negation, and so he negates it. He disappears, as the Hegelians say, as a consequence of his wisdom. He sees history as a whole, and so himself as a misery-producing error. His pride as a citizen or his human satisfaction is certainly not an adequate compensation for his misery. Finally, the wise man does not, most fundamentally, affirm the reason in history but the fact that a rational or well-ordered world is one without human self-consciousness. Only a world without history is one without contradiction, a system.

How could a self-conscious mortal, the being with time in him and nothing more, really be satisfied by political recognition? Fukuyama's attempt to defend this possibility against obvious criticisms is half-hearted and unconvincing, even to himself. The remaining contradictions are too clear, perhaps more clear than ever before. The coming of the universal and homogeneous state, the state with no credible opposition, makes more clear than ever before that there is no political or social solution to the problem of human individuality or self-consciousness.

So Kojève is right to say that the end of history would have to include man's rational self-destruction. He follows Rousseau in showing that man returns to a simple, natural existence, his beginning. So he agrees with Tocqueville that the universal and homogeneous state aims not to preserve the freedom and dignity of active citizens.[12] It means to replace politics by the automatic rule of automatons, or docile animals.[13] Human action is to be replaced by behavior as predictable and regular as that of any other animal.

The dissidents have shown us to our satisfaction that this reduction of human action and thought to systematic behavior was the aim of totalitarianism. They showed us what we already half-knew from writers such as Orwell. But Kojève adds that this "classless society" is the American as well as the Soviet aim. Solzhenitsyn and Havel at least almost agree, seeing it as the aim of modern rationalism as such. The spirit of resistance they affirm comes not from any rational or historical understanding of dignity, but from premodern sources, such as Christianity, that cause human beings to view themselves as immortal or eternal in some way.

Fukuyama, again, distinguishes himself by considering the end of history as a conceivably sustainable state full of human beings. He claims not to know why Kojève disagrees with Hegel by saying there will be no war or other form of human struggle at the end of history. War is caused by human desire, which will have disappeared. The "need for struggle" is what animated history. Absent the need, there will be no struggle.[14] Kojève's correction to Hegel here is on an Hegelian basis, and Fukuyama's inability to see why it was made shows that he has little idea of what the end of history *must* be like.

So Fukuyama is no wise man, and Kojève may be. Kojève affirms the end of history as a partisan of reason. He prefers a rational existence to the illusions or incomplete self-consciousness that supported various conceptions of human nature or human dignity. Fukuyama, in his eyes, would be like the dissidents or Tocqueville in preferring the illusions. Kojève never expressed any interest in or sympathy for Nietzsche's or Strauss's moralistic opposition to the "last man."[15] For him, it is or must be enough that the real is the rational, even if his moment of self-conscious wisdom is necessarily replaced by the simply unconscious or impersonal rule of reason. Strauss opposed the end of history because its coming would mean that philosophy would disappear from the world. For Kojève, Strauss forgets that the aim or *telos* of philosophy is to disappear, or to be replaced by wisdom.

According to Kojève, the wisdom available at the end of history is the only definitive or empirically verifiable atheism. Without that wisdom, philosophy itself is only a faith or prejudice. Those who speak of human nature cannot really be atheists. They lack the necessary evidence, and they cannot help but distinguish between man and God. Kojève knew as well as anyone that Strauss was not a believer in any conventional sense. But he still called him a theologian.[16]

Contrary to Fukuyama's equivocation, the fundamental alternative for Kojève is between those who speak of human nature and those who know that man is an essentially historical being. The former do not believe that history can come to an end, because they do not believe that human satisfaction could be simply historical. They do not believe that human beings can become wise, and they understand the distinction between man and God to be permanent.

Those who distinguish radically between nature and history hold open the possibility that man might transform or has transformed himself into a god. By so doing, he can prove to himself that there is no god but himself, and so also prove the truth of atheism. Kojève actually said that Kojève was a god, and that man at the end of history is somehow both divine and brutish. But such audacious and paradoxical statements do not find their way into Fukuyama's book.

Kojève also says that the wise man at the end of history is both divine and mortal. He is a particular individual in possession of divine or complete, universal science.[17] He must be divine, because he is no longer a man or the historical being who acts to transform his existence. He cannot be, at first glance, a brute, because he possesses the complete self-consciousness characteristic of God. But, from another perspective, he must be a brute, because he is mortal and unhistorical. What has happened is that human beings have lost their specifically human or historical attributes or acquisitions while retaining the physical or biological characteristics of their species. They live according to their nature, and so not according to their human or spiritual freedom from material determination.

It is still far from clear how man can be simultaneously divine and brutish, or how all I have just described can be simultaneously true. But we have already seen why we do well to search for a beginning of an explanation in Rousseau. He reported that his most choiceworthy condition, and his experience which was closest to man's uncorrupted or unhistorical nature, was a radical forgetfulness of his historical condition in an atemporal reverie.

Such reveries contained no awareness of time, mortality, or one's sociality. They are without, or almost without, what the human being acquired historically or over time. They include, in fact, "[n]othing external" to oneself. One's existence is radically solitary, but it includes all that exists. All there is is "[t]he sentiment of existence, stripped of every other emotion." "As long as this state lasts," Rousseau remembered, "we are sufficient unto ourselves, like God."[18]

The asocial individual who lives wholly in the present is not human or historical. He seems to be the brute of Rousseau's state of nature. But he is also divine in his self-sufficiency, including his genuine independence from other human beings. For him, it seems, everything is simultaneously divine and brutish. He experiences nothing external to himself. With the disappearance of history or human distinctiveness, all other distinctions disappear. What remains, as Tocqueville explained, is nothing but the experience of the truth of pantheism. Pantheism, Tocqueville understood, is the most seductive philosophy in modern or very self-conscious times. It is the complete negation of the misery of self-consciousness or individuality. Far more than any State or form of political organization, it is perfect in its universality and homogeneity.[19]

From the perspective of Kojève's wisdom, Rousseau's reveries at first seem very far from the end of history. Unlike Sartre, whom he classes among the "tasteless" existentialists,[20] he held that affirmation of history is not a reverie or diversion from the truth or self-consciousness. Kojève emphatically opposed the self-forgetfulness that can animate historical idealism, the attempt to lose oneself in the historical process. An account of history is simply an account of the truth, and so the human beings who live at the end of history can be perfectly self-conscious. The wise man lives wholly in the light of the truth, sees reveries for what they are, and has no interest in them.

Rousseau calls his reverie a "pleasurable fiction," a conscious negation of the truth about Rousseau in view of its misery. But to negate the truth one must know it. Rousseau's affirmation of the reverie is based on his theoretical conclusion that the wholly human or historical or social being is a miserable accident and nothing more. So his "fiction" is a response to a wisdom that anticipates the end of history.

Rousseau's "fiction," with its approximation of man's ahistorical beginning, is an approximation of man's genuine existence at the end of history. The end of history might almost be described as the universalization of Rousseau's extraordinarily asocial experience. In Kojève's time, the wise are wise because they see the whole of history as an error from the perspective of nature. In their divinity they affirm the universality of the experience of the brute's wholly natural existence. That experience—far more than the recognition all citizens receive in the universal and homogeneous state— is the self-sufficiency that man has always longed for and expressed in his conception of divinity. Both God and animal (or at least the self-sufficient, asocial being Rousseau describes in the state of nature) have no experience of time, and so at least very minimal social needs or dependence.

From this perspective, it is unsurprising that the wisdom of Rousseau would become especially clear at the time of the collapse of socialist idealism. The error of socialism was always that there could be a social solution to the problem of human disorder or dissatisfaction. The socialists, beginning with Marx, have always said that human beings will remain social and so human at the end of history. They have always viewed the end of history, like Fukuyama, as full of human beings. But if human beings remain human, they remain conscious of time, and so humanly miserable and dissatisfied. Contrary to Marx (and Fukuyama), the fundamental human scarcity is scarcity of time, and no amount of material prosperity can eradicate that scarcity. Human misery and, if Marx is right about its cause,[21] religion, will remain as long as human beings remain self-conscious mortals.

Generally speaking, Fukuyama's book is unconvincing because he knows too well the problems with the premise that human satisfaction could be both social and self-sufficient. As Rousseau shows, a social being simply is not a self-sufficient one. We have just suggested that material scarcity will not disappear as long as material desire is bloated by self-consciousness, as long as it is, in part, the feverish desire for luxury. Material scarcity will disappear, as Rousseau explained, only if material desire is reduced to its simply natural dimension, and so is satisfied quite easily or with hardly any work.

The desire for recognition, as the Christians see, seems really to be the desire for full and complete recognition, for a being who sees you as you really are. Social recognition, obviously, will always be partial. Human beings experience themselves as more than citizens, and their spirited desire to be recognized in their uniqueness will never be satisfied completely through social or political reform. Fukuyama says, quite rightly, that some will remain dissatisfied with merely receiving the recognition received equally by all. I would add that no human being would be fully satisfied, if only because the awareness that one's freedom depends upon intersubjective recognition is as much a recognition of dependence as of independence.

As Marx first noted in opposition to Hegel, the recognition of citizen by citizen seems particularly abstract in the modern world, the world of secularized Christianity. And as post-Hegelian or "postmodern" critics of many sorts observe, the modern State has not obliterated alienation, loneliness, restlessness anxiety, and so forth. Today's critics from Solzhenitsyn to Lyotard observe[22] that religious longings remain. They echo Tocqueville's account of American restlessness in the midst of prosperity and even the Marx of "On the Jewish Question."

Fukuyama knows, of course, that human beings are spirited or angry because they want to be free from their bodily limitations. But they want more than to win their freedom from fear in a life-risking struggle for pure prestige, the struggle that culminates in the universal freedom of citizens. They want actually to be immortal or eternal, or genuinely self-sufficient. The end of history freed from contingency and dependence reveals that there is no human satisfaction for the longing for immortality which, as Tocqueville says, equally torments every human heart.

Probably the obliteration of immortality or eternity as a human possibility, the end of all illusion, is what causes man's self-destruction at the end of history. That this possibility is not raised by Fukuyama suggests that he really believes that history has eradicated "religious" longing or focused it wholly on this world. But the destruction of socialism should have showed him that any theology of the historical liberation of human beings is untrue. Human beings will have religious longings as long as they remain human or social. Religion will not wither away unless man withers away.

Finally, the social basis of Fukuyama's view of the end of history seems to undermine the possibility of genuine wisdom. At the end of history, man is wise because he knows that history is all there is, and he comprehends history as an intelligible whole. But, in truth, he knows that history is not all there is. It is just all that he can comprehend, given the premise that man can only know what he can make, which is the historical or social world. But, in truth, it is not all he can comprehend. He also is aware of the contradiction between the historical and natural worlds, one which remains present in Kojève's thought that one can be both divine and mortal. As long as that contradiction remains inexplicable, man is not wise.

So the completion of human wisdom must be the thought that human distinctiveness must be negated. Kojève, the wise man, claims to know that man no longer exists. If Fukuyama is a wise man, or comprehends what it means for history to end, he must unequivocally reach the same conclusion. Fukuyama, from Kojève's perspective, is much less wise than reactionary, finally joining Nietzsche, Tocqueville, Havel, and so forth in preferring human liberty to the end of history. Fukuyama actually seems to regard the end of history as Kojève describes it as a future possibility to be resisted.

But if I have correctly described Fukuyama's lack of wisdom, then he compromises his partisanship fatally by calling liberal democracy the end of history. He does not clearly see liberal democracy as *limited* government. He sometimes knows that the principles of the universal and homogeneous State must inform all of human or social life for history to be over. He means to do justice to the Marxian criticism of a merely political and so merely abstract conclusion to history. Liberty in the sense of disorder or plurality must completely disappear. There is necessarily something totalitarian about this historical definition of liberty, something opposed to any idea of privacy or the transpolitical openness the American Framers left for conscience, or our duties to the Creator.

But Fukuyama, to repeat, also sometimes says that some room for irrationality and even religion must remain for the end of history to work. This incoherence comes as the result of his refinement of the Marxian thought that the end of history will be full of human beings with social desires. The end of history, unlike human liberty, cannot really be a struggle to perpetuate itself over time.

Kojève restored the wisdom of Rousseau against the Marxists by being perfectly aware of the incoherence of socialism, which is the same incoherence found in Fukuyama's description of liberal democracy as the end of history. He said that human beings cannot remain human, or conscious of time, at the end of history.[23] Today, perhaps this wisdom is in the process of becoming universalized. It is easy to see in the various forms of "postmaterialism," especially the ecological or New Age injunctions to live in harmony with nature. This pantheistic idealism, which is the view that history, in both its capitalist and socialist manifestations, is a nature-threatening disorder that must be extinguished in the name of health and security, is obviously more consistently posthistorical than its socialist predecessors. Postmaterialism really opposes the disorder that results from the mixing of material desire with self-consciousness. So it is actually *the* consistent materialism. It sees, as Rousseau did, that material scarcity will always be a human perception, no matter how much human beings produce, until human self-consciousness withers away.

Fukuyama is well aware of this growth in posthistorical wisdom, although he mistakenly presents it as evidence for the possibility that history has not come to an end after all. He notes, following Tocqueville (who, on this, followed Rousseau), that compassion, or secularized Christianity, grows in strength in the world. What really intensifies is the awareness that human beings, as such, are deserving of compassion and nothing more, because they are miserable accidents and nothing more.

This awareness, Fukuyama says, can be explained as a result of the working out over time of the consequences of modern science, which cannot distinguish qualitatively between human and non-human being. Hence it denies the genuine existence of human liberty or "moral choice." More precisely, from Fukuyama's perspective, modern science denies the existence of history, or the realm of human existence free from material determination.

But, if history has ended, modern science would now be completely true, even if it had not always been completely true. There can be no more human choices or action. What distinguishes human existence no longer exists. The contemporary inability to give an account of human dignity, or to find evidence of its genuine existence, might be the dawning of posthistorical awareness.

If there is no longer "any basis for saying that man has a superior dignity," then there is no longer any basis for man's conquest of or opposition to nature. This desire for consistency is what Fukuyama, following Tocqueville, calls "[t]he egalitarian passion that denies the existence of significant differences between human beings." He says it "can be extended to a denial of significant difference between man and the higher animals."[24] At the end of history, human distinctiveness is negated, and the laughably incoherent "animal rights" movement exists a moment before the nonexistence of rights.

This egalitarian line of thought, Fukuyama rightly says, opposes the idea that liberal democracy, animated by a "liberal concept of equal and universal humanity with a specifically human dignity" is the end of history. But it does not oppose the idea that history has ended. It aims at the consistent articulation of the end of history.

If liberal democracy is defensible, it is because history has not come to an end. It is because human beings remain human, between beast and God. It is because human beings are not essentially historical beings. They have longings which elude historical satisfaction. They point to some other foundation of moral choice or responsibility, one that opens human existence to eternity. The choice, it seems to me, is between the sober forms of this "postmodern" thought found, for example, in the thought of the dissidents, and the audacious vigor of Kojève's consistent articulation of the end of history, which expresses the culmination of the deepest modern aspirations. Fukuyama confuses us by not making this choice. He at least obscures both the brilliant plausibility of Kojève's analysis and the genuine greatness of both human liberty and liberal democracy.

Let me conclude by returning to the observation that Fukuyama assumes without proof that Kojève's atheism is true. He also assumes, without proof, that man can live well without God. He cannot think clearly about these assumptions because he does not really know whether man is a historical being, a being with a nature, or a created being. His lack of wisdom about the human condition ought to make him a very modest or pluralistic liberal, one devoted to a regime full of unwise and dissatisfied and so human beings. The dignity of man, he might have concluded, depends upon his elusiveness, and so upon his insurmountable resistance to systematic or scientific determination.

NOTES

1. Francis Fukuyama, *The End of History and the Last Man* (New York: The Free Press, 1992), p. 271. My essay is a criticism of one aspect of this book. Let me add here that there is much to admire in it, and that I am not doing justice here to what I learned from Fukuyama concerning contemporary affairs.

2. For an introduction to Solzhenitsyn's postmodernism, see his 1978 Harvard Commencement Address, "A World Split Apart," especially its conclusion, with his *Rebuilding Russia*, trans. A. Klimoff (New York: Farrar, Straus, and Giroux, 1991). On Havel, see his Address to the U.S. Congress (21 February 1990) with his "Politics and Conscience," *Open Letters: Selected Writing 1965–90*, trans. P. Wilson (New York: Knopf, 1990) and *Summer Meditations*, trans. P. Wilson (New York: Knopf, 1992).

3. See Alexandre Kojève, *Introduction to the Reading of Hegel*, ed. A. Bloom, trans. J. Nichols, Jr. (Ithaca: Cornell University Press, 1968), pp. 158–62, note 6 with Kojève, letter to Leo Strauss (19 September 1950) in Leo Strauss, *On Tyranny: Revised and Expanded Edition*, ed. V. Gourevitch and M. Roth (New York: Free Press, 1991), pp. 255–56.

   My understanding of Kojève's thought is greatly indebted to two intelligent and penetrating books: Michael S. Roth, *Knowing and History: Appropriations of Hegel in Twentieth Century France* (Ithaca: Cornell University Press, 1988) and especially Barry Cooper, *The End of History: An Essay on Modern Hegelianism* (Toronto: University of Toronto Press, 1984).

   The importance of the Strauss-Kojève correspondence for Fukuyama's book is obvious even in its title. Kojève argues for the end of history. Strauss is not convinced, calling attention, "for the sake of simplicity," to "Nietzsche's 'last man'" (Letter to Kojève, August 22, 1948, *On Tyranny*, p. 239).

4. Compare Fukuyama's account of a portion of Havel's "The Power of the Powerless" (pp. 166–69) with Havel's essay, found in *Open Letters*, as a whole. Consider, in particular, Fukuyama's sidestepping of what Havel means by the ideological denial of reality, an extreme manifestation of "living within the lie." This self-denial, for Havel, is

a perennial human temptation. Resisting this temptation is the foundation of what Fukuyama calls "moral choice" for Havel.

5. Fukuyama, pp. 138–39.

6. Fukuyama, pp. 162–65, 139.

7. Fukuyama, p. 364n7.

8. Fukuyama, p. 364n8, where Strauss's letter of 22 August 1948 is quoted. Fukuyama's use of this letter is confusing, because he does not actually quote or mention Strauss's key criticism.

9. See Rousseau, *Discourse on the Origin and Foundations of Inequality Among Men*. All my accounts of Rousseau's view of the relation between history and nature are based on this, his most theoretical, work.

10. Near the end of the *Discourse on Inequality*, Rousseau describes "the extreme point which closes the circle and touches the point from which we started. . . . Here all individuals become equals again because they are nothing." His conclusion is not quite expressed in Hegel's or Kojève's terms, but we can say that he anticipates what Marx and, more consistently, Kojève describe as the end of history. Perhaps we can say that Rousseau should have said that if the end is a return to the beginning, then it is return to the state of nature or the end of humanity. See Kojève, letter to Strauss (29 October 1953), *On Tyranny*, p. 262.

11. See Rousseau, *Discourse on Inequality*, Note i in light of Kojève, *Introduction*, Chapter 6. Almost all of the presentation of Kojève's view of the end of history as the end of human distinctiveness is based on this chapter. According to Kojève, "when specifically human error is finally transformed into the truth of absolute Science, Man ceases to exist as Man and History comes to an end. The overcoming of Man (that is, of Time, that is, of Action) in favor of static Being (that is, Space, that is, Nature), therefore, is the overcoming of Error in favor of Truth" (p. 156).

12. Alexis de Tocqueville, *Democracy in America*, volume 2, part 4, chapter 6 in the context of volume 2 as a whole.

13. Kojève, letter to Strauss (19 September 1950), p. 255.

14. Fukuyama, p. 389n1.

15. Note the absence of this interest or sympathy in his letters to Strauss.

16. Roth, p.134n22: "In Kojève's copy of the typescript of Strauss's lecture 'What is Political Philosophy,' Kojève wrote 'Strauss = Theology,' alongside Strauss's discussion of political theology."

17. See Cooper, p. 274.

18. Rousseau, *Reveries of a Solitary Walker*, Walk 5.

19. Tocqueville, *Democracy*, volume 2, part 1, chapter 7.

20. Kojève, letter to Strauss (29 October 1953), p. 262.

21. See Marx, "Critique of Hegel's *Philosophy of Right*" with his "On the Jewish Question." The latter shows that the Americans living the universal and homogenous state remain religious because they experience their true or human existence as miserably whimsical.

22. On Lyotard's defense of religious longing against Kojève's systematic rationalism, see Thomas L. Pangle, *The Ennobling of Democracy* (Baltimore: John Hopkins University Press, 1992), pp. 20–33, 48–56.

23. See Kojève, *Introduction*, 154–66, especially note 6.

24. Fukuyama, pp. 297–98.

8

The Federalist's Hostility to Leadership
and the Crisis of the Contemporary Presidency

We are in the midst of yet another contemporary crisis of presidential leadership. President Reagan's scarcely stunning but nonetheless very real success for almost five years was a cause for wonder. His self-destruction was expected, because presidents of late usually fail. The "teflon" was protecting Reagan not so much from his idiosyncratic weaknesses as from the fate of contemporary presidents.

We clearly have demanded too much from recent presidents. We surely hold them too personally responsible for our moral and political well-being.[1] The origin of this demand is found in the best thinkers of the progressive era, who were profoundly and indignantly dissatisfied with how little was demanded from or possible for presidential leadership in their time. Woodrow Wilson's thought, in particular, is the primary source of the contemporary opinion concerning the necessity of popular leadership for a successful presidency.[2]

By leadership Wilson meant some combination of personal integrity, oratorical skill, and democratic moral vision that would make the president *the* articulator of American political principle. A leader, when acting as a leader, does not descend into the details of administration or build coalitions of interest groups. He leads by forming and reforming a people by articulating their moral aspirations. The democratic accountability and unity of the presidency allows the president, as a person, to represent America as a moral whole. The leader embodies the people's principles, and he unites the people into one political body through oratorical eloquence. This unity, properly understood, overcomes the demoralizing tendency of the Constitution to oppose the idea of national political community through the separation of powers.[3]

Wilson tended to view personal, presidential leadership as a replacement for the impersonal rule of the Constitution. Constitutional attachments and, in fact, all fixed political principles oppose the leader's visionary promotion of progressive political change. Such attachments are, in effect, ways of deferring to the leadership of individuals now dead and gone, and to principles which are not relevant to today's circumstances. Wilson's Darwinian idea of political evolution is meant to suggest that constitutionalism is reactionary. It deprives the people of today of the opportunity to be ennobled by their leaders, to be formed according to their own aspirations.[4]

The myth of constitutional deference, when accepted by American presidents, is, in truth, a reflection of their timidity and their lack of leadership. To give them more boldness, Wilson attempted to replace this myth with another. The Constitution, he contends, evolves with all the other forces of life; its meaning is in a constant process of reinterpretation. The leader ought to be the primary interpreter. Consequently, there is no constitutional impediment to the president attempting to become "as big a man as he can" for his own and the common good.[5] He certainly ought to be big enough not to defer to the limits on leadership established by the Constitution's framers.

Because of the Constitution's continuing power, American presidents, despite the partial success of Wilson's project, are not yet liberated leaders. They do not yet rule without impediment simply by articulating success-fully the people's common aspirations. Some reformers today still want to see the Wilsonian project completed. They call for constitutional reform to give the president more of "the power to lead."[6]

But perhaps we have already seen enough of the Wilsonian project to say that it is no longer reasonable to hope for its success. Oratory already plays an important and growing part in presidential politics, including presidential selection. The presidency has become more personal, and the opportunities for leadership seem greater. Despite or because of these changes, we have seen, if anything, a decline in the quality of presidential leadership and presidential effectiveness. It is widely perceived, and not because of Reagan, that we are in the midst of a "crisis of competence."[7] Experience has at least partially discredited Wilson's project to discredit the Constitution's limitations on presidential leadership. It is time for reasons other than Bicentennial piety to give the original understanding of the Constitution's relationship to political leadership a fresh hearing. I will contribute to this project by an analysis of *The Federalist*'s argument defending the Constitution's hostility to leadership.

The Federalist's **Leader**

The term leader is employed in *The Federalist* sparingly but with an almost uncanny precision.[8] In agreement with Wilson and his disciples today, *The Federalist* understands the Constitution to establish an "anti-leadership system."[9] Its purpose is to resist the imposition of innovations proposed by leaders. *The Federalist*, unlike Wilson, affirms this resistance, because it is considerably less sanguine than Wilson about the motivations and likely consequences of the success of democratic leaders. Like Wilson again, *The Federalist* emphasizes oratorical skill as they key talent of a leader in a democracy. This talent is used by the leader to arouse popular passions on behalf of a political purpose or vision. For Wilson, this arousal of popular feeling, presented as feeling *with* the people, is for the purpose of moral elevation. *The Federalist* describes it as seduction, or moral destruction through the cynical manipulation of popular feeling.[10] *The Federalist*'s leader, Wilson would say, is not truly a leader, because he is lacking in moral integrity and popular sympathy. *The Federalist* would say that Wilson's leader is an ideal too rarely found in reality to be relied upon by partisans of self-government.[11]

The inevitable presence of leaders in a free, democratic regime is presented by *The Federalist* as perhaps the most important reason for thinking that the belief in the possibility of political harmony in America without a strong union held together by institutions with teeth in them is utopian.[12] The cause of political discord is faction, and "[t]he latent causes of faction . . . are sown in the nature of man." Leaders are always "factious leaders." They create political organization by appealing to the passions and interests that unite some human beings in a way "adverse to the rights of other citizens or to the permanent and aggregate interests of the community."[13]

The causes of factious selfishness in human nature are all rooted in the fact that human beings are self-conscious and embodied; they are individuals.[14] The self-assertiveness flowing from the naturalness of self-love in its most extreme or most political manifestation is the cause of leadership. A leader not presently in power is a reformer because he prefers his own forms; he cannot be satisfied unless he rules. His innovative moralism, even his visionary utopianism, are primarily his plans for imposing *himself* on the world.[15]

Revolutionary Leaders

The Federalist, recognizing the universality of the connection between reason and self-love, cannot be so moralistic as to dismiss leadership out of hand. It praises the "leaders of the [American] Revolution."[16] It suggests, by so doing, that those outstanding individuals were not motivated primarily by disinterested idealism, but their partisanship on behalf of the revolutionary idealism still coincided with the people's true interests. This self-assertion of these "patriotic leaders" formed the American people into an "enthusiastic" whole, replacing "the ordinary diversity" of factionalism with extraordinary national unity. The resulting "universal resentment against the ancient government" destroyed the traditional or customary impediments to the construction of a regime based upon "reflection and choice."[17]

The Federalist also praises the boldness of revolutionary leadership when opposing those who fear that the Constitution's "extended republic" is too innovative or experimental. It praises the "manly spirit" of those who will not rest content with given forms, and those who will not accept blindly decisions made by others. When speaking of the American founding, *The Federalist* says the "new" course is "more noble." The fact that both the Revolution and the Constitution were partly experimental deviations from experience makes them more problematic and more admirable, more products of human reflection and choice, than they would have been if they followed without thought or risk the models tested by others.[18]

Leaders and the Constitution

The Federalist suggests that the Constitution itself is a self-assertion very similar to leadership. The authors of *The Federalist* are very reticent concerning their own motivation for their support of the Constitution, but they do affirm the nobility of being ruled by the desire for fame, the most elevated form of political ambition.[19] This ambition, however noble, is ambition nonetheless. The Constitution, as an honorable, unprecedented experiment in self-government, depends for its origination and success upon individuals who are at least closely akin to great leaders.[20] This honor or even a greatness of soul that goes beyond honor may take the authors of *The Federalist* beyond the vulgar concern for success at whatever cost that characterizes leadership in its pure form, but perhaps not too far beyond.[21]

One thing, and arguably the most telling thing, that separates the extended, diverse republic created by the Constitution from previous democratic experiments is the likelihood of its long duration. According to *The Federalist*, the reason popular government has suffered from a bad reputation is its instability, which caused human beings to feel insecure about their lives, liberty and property, about whatever they justly call their own.[22] Perhaps what raises the authors of *The Federalist* above leaders and leadership is their recognition of the transience of oratorical victories. Their passion for fame or long-term victory caused them to communicate carefully in writing about the effectual protection of rights, in words that are intended to endure the test of time.[23]

The Federalist hopes and expects that the American people will continue to support and respect the Constitution, and hence the wisdom of its framers. The people will do so partly because they will see that the Constitution really serves to protect their rights. But the Constitution will also acquire the "veneration which time bestows on everything" which shows extraordinary resistance to the forces of change. Such "veneration" is indiscriminate, and strictly speaking, cannot be affirmed by rational and honorable human beings. It would not be appropriate for "a nation of philosophers."[24] It seems inevitable that Constitutional veneration would find enemies in leaders with philosophical pretensions, such as Woodrow Wilson.

The heart of Wilson's dissatisfaction with the Constitution is in its intention to discipline the thought or vision of American leaders by making them affirm the Constitution's principles if they are to be effective. Even President Wilson to some large extent was subordinated to the framers' wisdom. The perpetuation of the American or any other Constitution requires the constraint and even the discrediting of leaders and leadership.[25] American leaders operating under constitutional constraints cannot help but envy the opportunities for greatness that were given to the leaders of the Revolution and the framers by their extra-constitutional circumstances. They also cannot help but believe that their real, personal excellence deserves to replace constitutional prejudice in the people's hearts.

But even Wilson realized that most human beings are not inclined to be philosophers.[26] No amount of leadership can remedy that situation. Given the inevitability of prejudice, *The Federalist* affirms the Americans' prejudice in favor of their Constitution, because it supports a reasonable form of government.

Constitutional veneration, *The Federalist* expects, will engender a salutary, spirited resistance to the leader-produced idea of the necessity or desirability of constitutional change. This resistance still is strong enough that it has only been partially undermined by generations of "progressive" leadership. Even today, almost all parties agree the idea of radical constitutional reform in the interest of liberated leadership seems an impossible dream in America.[27] To a very large extent, the Constitution's framers still rule America today.

When discussing America after the Constitution is in place, *The Federalist* displays nothing but hostility toward the "experiments" that "may be produced . . . by the ambition of enterprising leaders,"[28] because the time when the passion for political experimentation is salutary is over. Boldness is appropriately replaced by caution, and the conclusion that "the [successful] experiments [of the American people during the founding period] are of too ticklish a nature to be unnecessarily multiplied" is in order.[29] The human qualities that work for the maintenance of the well-designed institutions of a good Constitution are to be encouraged in preference to those favorable to the always dangerous instability promoted by leadership.[30]

Leaders are useful for protecting the Constitution from other leaders or would-be tyrants. The inevitability of their presence in a free, popular regime causes *The Federalist* not to be overly concerned with the threat of executive tyranny. The jealousy or resentment of leaders aid Congress in effectively checking the president on behalf of republican liberty, in performing one of its legitimate constitutional functions.[31]

But the attacks of leaders are primarily threats to constitutional order. A leader will oppose all exercises of executive power, simply because they are not his own, especially those which serve to satisfy the people by protecting their rights. His intention, after all, to lead the people to feel that their rights are threatened and revolution is in order. When their rights are not, in fact, being threatened, which *The Federalist* holds would ordinarily be the case under the American Constitution, then he must mislead or deceive them.[32]

The leader's apparent zeal in defense of the people's rights is always an instrument for his own rule. If the people's rights are, in fact, being threatened, he acts well, although not for disinterested motives. When they are not threatened, he acts badly. The better a Constitution functions, the more his self-interest and his activity become political treachery.[33]

Leaders and Presidential Power

The Constitution creates a strong presidency, in part, to ensure that the president will be a partisan of the Constitution. The combination of a long, fixed term and the possibility of reeligibility through popular approval allows him and inspires him to pursue projects in the people's and the Constitution's long-term interests, even against popular "inclinations" or impulsive "temporary delusions" almost surely enflamed by the "arts" of "flatter[ing]" leaders. His hoped-for reward will be immortal glory, which the people reserve for those who have resisted their inclinations for their own good. He wants "lasting monuments" erected in honor of his "courage and magnanimity." Fame will be available to statesmen who use their Constitutional powers extraordinarily well (but not to leaders) under the Constitution. Consequently, the noblest form of ambition need not turn American presidents into revolutionaries.[34]

Constructive presidential "leadership," which *The Federalist* does not call leadership,[35] protects the Constitution or the effectual protection of rights against the destructiveness of leaders who otherwise might fatally mislead the people and hence dominate legislatures, which receive their energy primarily from popular inclinations and will be an inviting home for leaders and oratory. *The Federalist* trusts in the people's ability to make long-term, deliberate judgments concerning their interests. It does not trust in public opinion however understood. The people judge well when they reflect on the results of government policy; they judge badly on the basis of oratorical appeals. *The Federalist* trusts the people to judge deeds, not words.

Presidential elections ordinarily ought to be referenda on the effectiveness of the administration in power. The long, fixed term gives the president the reasonable hope that projects begun early in his term will have time enough to succeed well enough for the people to appreciate their beneficial results, for his firm actions to speak louder than his opponents' words. Eventually, and quite properly, the president is accountable to the people, but only for his real successes and failures.[36]

The Federalist calls upon the president to rule not through the rhetorical management of public opinion, but through the effective use of his constitutional power.[37] The Constitution, by insulating him from short-term doubts and doubters, will habituate the people to trust in his decisive judgment. Without its restraints on the people's inevitable propensity to have a leader-enflamed prejudice against executive power, the president would lack the "energy" which is an indispensable part of all good government. It is often forgotten today that the separation of powers works to support more than to detract from presidential decisiveness.[38]

The Federalist's support of the executive energy is on behalf of "good government," whatever its form. All political choices are merely political theory unless effectually implemented.[39] *The Federalist* understands the American people to have chosen liberal democracy, a democracy which protects the rights of minorities. The president resists short-term, illiberal majoritarianism because he believes that a reflective or truly self-conscious majority will be a liberal one. His "leadership," he believes, will be affirmed once it dispels the delusions of leadership.

This resistance to transient majoritarianism has produced the "progressive" opinion that *The Federalist*'s opposition to presidential leadership is anti-democratic. This opinion produced the "new Hamiltonianism" of the progressive understanding of the presidency, which receives its energy from popular leadership. This opinion, in truth, is misleading. Its clarity or simplicity is achieved by obscuring Hamilton's appreciation of the problematic character of democracy.[40] *The Federalist*, when contemplating possibilities for majority tyranny, thinks of the poor exploiting the rich, as would today's conservatives, but it also thinks of racism and religiously-inspired moral majoritarianism, as would today's liberals. When it thinks of leaders, it calls to mind those who would exploit any of these tyrannic impulses, and it understands the presidency as a check on such leadership. Leaders who claim authority to rule simply through their articulation of the people's inclinations cannot have their way in a *liberal* democracy.

When today's liberals praise presidential leadership, they think of Franklin Roosevelt and Lyndon Johnson, of presidents forming majorities on behalf of "social justice," which primarily means the expansion of the welfare state. Opposition to this expansion, they believe, comes from the self-interest of oligarchs masquerading under an obsolete understanding of rights. A self-conscious majority, one enlightened by leadership, is thought to be characteristically a "progressive" one. These liberals see this majoritarianism as superior to constitutionalism, and they do not acknowledge sufficiently the possibility that, even with constitutional restraints, ill-considered and unjust economic programs have sometimes been put into effect by liberal majorities formed by liberal leaders, programs which the majority reasonably came later to regret. Today's liberals have tended to be so certain of the justice of progressive programs that they have not seen the goodness of constitutionally-inspired and empowered resistance to their immediate implementation.[41]

But what happens when liberalism is no longer majoritarianism? Liberals view the effective leadership of Ronald Reagan as deception or seduction of the majority through the "Great Communicator's" personal charm. They have rediscovered the virtues of institutional restraints which prevent the ill-considered implementation of Reagan's more radical proposals. Conservatives, meanwhile, now praise presidential leadership and are vigorously opposing anti-majoritarian theories of constitutional interpretation.[42]

Leadership and Oratory

Leadership more forcefully opposes than supports effective executive action on behalf of the Constitution. Leaders or orators are more effective when they are negative, because it is harder, in public debate, to defend accomplishments and plans than to attack them. The leader's preferred method of enhancing his own reputation is the oratorical destruction of the reputation of those who hold power. His partisanship manifests itself most readily and effectively in an indignant campaign "against Washington," in an angry populism distrustful of all government and governors. According to *The Federalist*, the "noble enthusiasm for liberty," especially when aroused by leaders, "is apt to be infected with a spirit of narrow and illiberal distrust."[43] Opportunities for and the legitimation of the idea of leadership tend to favor the president's opponents, as they favored the King's opponents during the Revolution.

The Federalist, because it doubts that oratory could be an important component of constructive yet limited or constitutional rule, would not be surprised that the presidency is in crisis today. More than anything else, the partial legitimation of the idea of leadership has empowered negative campaigns, and its most conspicuous product is one failed presidency after another. Today's liberal reformers should have had enough experience to see that there is a deep tension between their call for a more energetic executive and their assertion that this energy must be rooted in popular leadership. The last president to leave office with the respect of the American people for his "leadership" was Eisenhower, whose "hidden-hand" method of governing owed almost nothing to popular oratorical persuasion.[44]

Wilson, in a very aristocratic fashion, understands oratory to be a revelation of excellence of character, and, in a very democratic fashion, he trusts in the people's ability to make good judgments concerning such revelations. He affirms a variant of the Jeffersonian belief that the people, given proper conditions, will choose the natural *aristoi* of talent and virtue to lead them.[45] If debates about fundamental political principles between those competing for political power occur unimpeded and in the open, the people will not be deceived. Wilson seems to doubt that intellectual sophistry and "image making" can hide effectively the reality of the person's character.[46]

The Federalist tends to identify oratory with demagoguery, the forming of majority factions to oppress minority rights.[47] Oratory, or at least successful oratory, is typically seductive or shameless. In a public debate, the honorable statesman, who is capable of feeling shame and hence will not say anything to win, will be typically defeated by a shameless manipulator. Such a shameless orator is usually able to hide his character from his audience. A democratic audience is particularly easy to seduce.[48]

The Federalist recommends the diversity of the extended commercial republic as a barrier to political communication and hence to the oratorical formation of a majority faction. "The influence of factious leaders may kindle a flame within their particular states, but will be unable to spread a general conflagration through the other states."[49] The Constitution does not seek to eradicate leaders and leadership, because that could not be done without eliminating liberty or diversity. Instead, it attempts to make leaders as weak as possible by denying them opportunities for oratorical success.

Crisis Leadership

In times of genuine crisis, which the Constitution intends to make very rare, presidential leadership, or a statesmanship very akin to leadership, is indispensable. In fulfillment of his oath, the president must do whatever is required to protect the Constitution, and his ability to use ordinarily unconstitutional means depends more on his popular support than on respect for his constitutional position.[50] The president might have the incentive to create crises, especially in foreign policy. But the constitutional powers given to Congress are meant to be strong enough to prevent, at least usually, crisis provocation in the interest of leadership.

Recent presidents, believing that they must be leaders to be effective, have become partisans of crisis. They have tended to believe that they must forcefully call the people's attention to critical situations to accomplish the requisite political reform. The thought is that because the Constitution no longer sufficiently empowers the president to confront successfully the challenges he faces, he must turn more and more to leading or the oratorical molding of public opinion as a source of power.[51]

Since Herbert Hoover, presidents have used the language of war to describe domestic emergencies, and they have characteristically exaggerated the extent of domestic dangers to the well-being of Americans.[52] Franklin Roosevelt "claimed that the battles of the New Deal were as important and deep as the battles of the Civil War."[53] Lyndon Johnson declared "war on poverty," asserting that the critical struggle would not be over until poverty, like the Japanese and the Germans, had surrendered unconditionally.[54] Jimmy Carter called the energy crisis "the moral equivalent of war," requiring a war-like national commitment and self-sacrifice.[55]

These attempts at crisis recognition or creation have not been simply generated by perceptions of national necessity. Presidents have come to think it their duty to raise Americans above the "ordinary diversity" of materialistic self-interest through Wilsonian moral leadership. They have attempted to create the national unity based on a feeling of national purpose that only crisis (or, as *The Federalist* says, revolutionary) leadership can provide.[56]

The indiscriminate use of the idea of crisis is the source of the two qualities which have been often used to describe the oratory of the "rhetorical" or "personal," "plebiscitary" presidency: overuse and oversell.[57] The people have tended to react appropriately, with increasing boredom and cynicism, and the seemingly inevitable rhetorical excesses of recent presidents have made them easy targets for opposition leaders. The overall result has been a decrease in presidential power and effectiveness, and even a degradation of the moral force of presidential rhetoric. The Constitution, as well as the nature of leadership itself, ensure that oratorical crisis-provocation cannot be a reliable source of presidential power.

The Moralism of Leaders

The Federalist's opposition to leadership is part of its general distrust of "moral and religious motives" as instruments of effective government for the protection of rights.[58] Such motives are sometimes admirable, and, without a doubt, they, in a highly refined form, are parts of a human excellence that surpasses politics altogether.[59]

But such motives usually manifest themselves politically as what we call "moralism," or indignant assertion of rule by virtue of some quality of soul. *The Federalist* describes such assertions as a source of political conflict as "animosity," or soul-based hatred. Moral and religious motives point more powerfully toward tyranny than toward the just self-restraint implied in the idea of constitutional morality. They readily produce the desire to dominate the souls of others to confirm the worth of one's own soul. They are rarely the source of personal moderation flowing from a devotion to the Constitution or the idea of human liberty. Because human beings are rather easily "inflamed . . . with mutual animosity," they "are much more disposed to vex and oppress each other than to cooperate for their common good."[60]

A leader is motivated himself by and appeals to the people's animosity. He is angry that the excellence of his own soul has received insufficient political recognition, and he attempts to persuade the people that the government also means to degrade them. His oratory also means to degrade the souls of those who do not share in his innovative idealism. He does everything he can to generate soul-based controversy. He intends to put the people in a mood resistant to compromise and a just regard for the legitimacy of the diverse opinions of others.

Leadership appeals to that part of human nature that makes diversity irritating or even hateful as a manifestation of the limits of one's own moral excellence. The moralism of leadership defies the proper limits to government, in its "charismatic" propensity to attempt to overcome the limits intrinsic to human nature. As far as possible, constitutional government should not be thought to require the political elevation of citizens' souls, especially through leadership.[61]

A Constitution operating under this injunction might be interpreted not to do justice to the desire of a free people for political invigoration.[62] But it is more likely that the genius of the Constitution, as articulated in *The Federalist*, is its self-conscious institutionalization of the tension between leadership and constitutionalism. This tension reflects human nature in its diversity, and has given America much of its genuinely liberal and democratic vitality. Because leaders can take care of themselves, and do not have to be given constitutional incentives to do so, *The Federalist* may have wisely taken the case of the Constitution against leadership to an extreme. Extremism in defense of liberty is no vice, and it has not prevented the emergence of statesmen such as Lincoln, FDR, and Lyndon Johnson (on civil rights), of characters which *The Federalist*'s analysis of human nature, strictly speaking, cannot comprehend.[63]

Recent presidents have typically expected more from popular leadership than is reasonable. It has been shown time and again not to provide enough support to energize more than a small part of a president's term. Most of the time, leaders and leadership, as *The Federalist* predicted, have been the president's enemies. A president, even today, has every incentive to expect more from the Constitution than from leadership and to teach others, more by example than by oratory, to respect the constitutional foundation of his office's powers and responsibilities.

NOTES

1. See Theodore Lowi, *The Personal Presidency* (Ithaca: Cornell University Press, 1985).

2. According to Jeffrey Tulis: "The modern doctrine of presidential leadership was consciously formulated and put into place by Woodrow Wilson" ("The Decay of Presidential Rhetoric," *Rhetoric and American Statesmanship*, ed. G. Thurow and J. Wallin [Durham: Carolina Academic Press, 1984], p. 107).

   Other sources to which I am indebted which emphasize Wilson's theoretical contribution to the twentieth century reform of the presidency and the American idea of leadership include: James Ceaser, *Presidential Selection* (Princeton: Princeton University Press, 1979) and Charles Kesler, "Woodrow and the Statesmanship of Progress," in *Natural Right and Political Right*, ed. T. Silver and P. Schramm (Durham: Carolina Academic Press, 1984), pp. 103–28.

3. Wilson, *Constitutional Government in the United States* (New York: Columbia University Press, 1908), pp. 54–71.

4. Consider that in his book on constitutional government Wilson begins his chapter on the presidency with a discussion of the truth of the Darwinian understanding of the nature of politics (*ibid.*, p. 54).

5. *Ibid.*, p. 70.

6. James MacGregor Burns, *The Power to Lead* (New York: Simon and Schuster, 1984), pp. 235–38.

   According to Burns, there is "a wealth of potential leadership ready to burst through present constraints . . . built into the system" (101–02).

7. See James Sundquist, "Congress, the President, and the Crisis of Competence in Government," *Congress Reconsidered*, ed. L. C. Dodd and B. I. Oppenheimer (Washington: Congressional Quarterly Press, 1981), pp. 351–70.

8. Alexander Hamilton, John Jay, and James Madison, *The Federalist* (New York: The Modern Library, n.d.).

    I realize that the use of *The Federalist* for determining the intentions of the framers of the Constitution is not unproblematic, especially concerning the presidency. Herbert Storing makes the relevant point where he says: "*The Federalist* brings the creation of the Presidency to completion, so far as the founding generation was concerned" ("Introduction" to Charles C. Thach, Jr., *The Creation of the Presidency* [Baltimore: Johns Hopkins University Press, 1969], p. xii.).

    The places where "leaders," and "leading" are found in *The Federalist* are given in T. S. Engeman, E. J. Erler, and T. B. Hofsteller, eds., *The Federalist Concordance* (Middletown, Conn.: Wesleyan University Press, 1979), p. 295.

    The peculiar, precise use of these terms discussed in this essay was first noted by Robert Eden. See his *Political Leadership and Nihilism* (Tampa: University Presses of Florida, 1983). Ceaser, acknowledging a debt to Eden, makes good use of these terms in his *Presidential Selection*, pp. 52-61. Neither of these two fine books provides a comprehensive analysis of *The Federalist*'s leader, but I owe large debts to both of them.

9. Burns, p. 15.

10. See *The Federalist* 62, p. 403. See Eden, p. 5.

11. See Ceaser, *Presidential Selection*, pp. 182–83, 194–95.

12. *Federalist* 6, pp. 27–29.

13. *Federalist* 10, pp. 54–55, 61. See Eden, p. 3.

14. See *ibid.*, p. 55 on the causes of faction.

15. See *Federalist* p. 27 with David F. Epstein, *The Political Theory of 'The Federalist'* (Chicago: University of Chicago Press, 1984), pp. 71–72 and Machiavelli on the "new prince," *The Prince*, Chapter 6.

16. *Federalist* 14, p. 85.

17. *Federalist* 49, p. 320; *Federalist* 1, p. 3.

18. *Federalist* 14, p. 85; Epstein, pp. 112–13.

19. *Federalist* 1, p. 6; *Federalist* 72, p. 370.

20. See Epstein, p. 124.

21. Paul Eidelberg, *A Discourse on Statesmanship* (Urbana: University of Illinois Press, 1974), pp. 241–78.

22. *Federalist* 10, p. 58.

23. Consider James MacGregor Burns, *Leadership* (New York: Harper and Row, 1978), p. 454.

24. *Federalist* 49, pp. 328–29. Consider *Federalist* 14's criticism of "a blind veneration for antiquity" (p. 85).

25. Consider Burns, *Leadership*, p. 454: "It was ironic that . . . [the framers'] brilliant leadership would found a system that so hobbled leadership." This irony the framers viewed as a necessity.

26. One Wilsonian statement on the problem of modern government: "The bulk of mankind is rigidly unphilosophical, and nowadays the bulk of mankind votes" ("The Study of Administration," in *Basic Literature of American Public Administration 1787–1950*, ed. F. Mosher [New York: Holmes and Meier, 1981], p. 73).

27. Consider for example the "pessimistic note" that concludes Sundquist's chapter on "The Prospects for Constitutional Reform" (*Constitutional Reform and Effective Government* [Washington, D.C.: The Brookings Institution, 1986]).

28. *Federalist* 43, pp. 282–83.

29. *Federalist* 49, p. 320.

30. See Herbert Storing, "American Statesmanship: Old and New," *Bureaucrats, Policy Analysts, Statesmen: Who Leads?* ed. R. Goldwin (Washington: American Enterprise Institute, 1980), p. 98 and Eden, p. xv.

31. See Ceaser, *Presidential Selection*, p. 53. See also *Federalist* 66, p. 435.

32. See *Federalist* 1, pp. 5–6.

33. See *Federalist* 59, p. 387.

34. *Federalist* 71 and 72, pp. 463–74.

35. For able discussions of *The Federalist*'s promotion of presidential leadership given in apparent ignorance of its idiosyncratic use of the term, see Harvey Flaumenhaft, "Hamilton's Administrative Republic and the American Presidency," *The Presidency in the Constitutional Order*, ed. J. Bessette and J. Tulis (Baton Rouge: LSU Press, 1981), pp. 95–99 and Jeffrey Sedgwick, "Executive Leadership and Administration: Founding Versus Progressive Views," *Administration and Society* 17 (February 1986), pp. 411–32.

36. *Federalist* 71, p. 467 and *Federalist* 72, pp. 469–70.

37. *Federalist* 72, pp. 479–70.

38. See Sundquist, *Constitutional Reform*, p. 68 with Flaumenhaft, p. 96.

39. *Federalist* 70, p. 454.

40. According to Herbert Croly, the purpose of progressive reform in favor of nationalism and presidential power was to give "democratic meaning and purpose to Hamiltonian tradition and method" (*The*

Promise of American Life [New York: E. P. Dutton, 1909], p. 169). See Storing, "American Statesmanship," p. 96.

41. The classic statement of this position is James Sundquist, *Politics and Policy: The Eisenhower, Kennedy, and Johnson Years* (Washington, D.C.: Brookings, 1968).

42. Here it would be sufficient to mention Attorney General Ed Meese. See the instructively extreme call for conservative presidential leadership by Reagan, complete with a sophisticated constitutional argument, in Douglas A. Jeffrey, "The Iran-*contra* Affair and the Real Crisis of American Government," *The Claremont Review* 5 (Spring, 1987), pp. 3–9.

   For a reasonable, largely unheeded call for conservatives to use their success to replace populism, especially presidential populism, with a revival of constitutionalism, see Harvey Mansfield, Jr., "The American Electorate: Towards Constitutional Democracy?" *Government and Opposition* 16 (Winter, 1981), pp. 1–18.

43. *Federalist* 1, p. 3. See Ceaser, *Presidential Selection*, pp. 246–59.

   For an interpretation of the implementation of primary-oriented reforms as the institutionalization of the progressive La Follette's politics of indignation, see my "Robert Marion La Follette, Sr." *American Political Orators in the Twentieth Century*, ed. B. Duffy and H. Ryan (Westport, CT: Greenwood Press, 1987), pp. 281–82.

44. See Paul Johnson, *Modern Times* (New York: Harper & Row, 1983), pp. 461–64. The phrase "hidden-hand" Johnson, of course, borrows from Fred Greenstein.

45. See Jefferson, letter to John Adams (October 28, 1813).

46. See Ceaser, *Presidential Selection*, p. 61.

47. See especially *Federalist* 10, p. 58.

48.   See James Ceaser et al., "The Rise of the Rhetorical Presidency," *Rethinking the Presidency*, ed. T. Cronin (Boston: Little, Brown & Co., 1982), p. 238.

49.   *Federalist* 10, p. 61. See *Federalist* 85, p. 568.

50.   See *Federalist* 23, p. 142.

51.   See, for example, the moderate statement of this position at the conclusion of Elmer Cornwell, *Presidential Leadership of Public Opinion* (Bloomington: Indiana University Press, 1965), p. 303.

52.   See Johnson, pp. 244–60.

53.   John Zvesper, "The Liberal Rhetoric of Franklin Roosevelt," in Thurow and Wallin, ed., p. 90.

54.   See Lyndon Johnson, State of the Union Address (January 8, 1964).

55.   For a measured account of the relationship between Carter's moralism and his rhetoric, see Michael J. Malbin, "Rhetoric and Leadership: A Look Backward at the Carter Energy Plan," *Both Ends of the Avenue*, ed. A. King (Washington: American Enterprise Institute, 1983), pp. 212–45.

56.   See Lyndon Johnson, "The Great Society," Commencement Address at the University of Michigan (May 22, 1964) as an oratorical effort to raise Americans above "soulless wealth" for public virtue.

57.   See Ceaser et al., p. 247 and Lowi, pp. 134–75.

58.   *Federalist* 10, p. 9.

59.   See my "James Madison and the Metaphysics of Modern Politics," *Review of Politics* 48 (January, 1986), pp. 92–115.

60. *Federalist* 10, p. 56. Also see the connection between animosity and intolerance in *Federalist* 1, pp. 3–4.

61. See Sedgwick, pp. 416–17.

62. See Storing, "American Statesmanship," p. 98 and W. C. McWilliams et al., "The Constitution and the Education of Citizens," unpublished manuscript.

63. See Storing, "American Statesmanship," pp. 98–100.

9

The Constitutional Presidency of George Bush

The 1992 presidential election, as Bill Clinton predicted, was mostly a simple vote for change, for anyone but the incumbent. This "negative landslide" showed most clearly that President Bush had a woefully inadequate understanding of how to use his power in order to preserve it. His theory of presidential power was, in key ways, too constitutional. That is one way of saying it was not democratic enough. It is also a way of saying that Bush seemed insufficiently devoted to the revolutionary principle that animates democratic government even under the Constitution. The president did not understand that even constitutional government must be defended by principle.

Bush's theory of presidential power, of what the president can and ought to accomplish in his constitutional role, can be viewed as part of *The Federalist*'s defense of the Constitution against revolutionary innovation or disorder. This defense has been revived in recent years by constitutionalist scholars in criticism of the emergence of the "rhetorical presidency," which the Framers clearly did not intend.[1] Without claiming to know whether President Bush was influenced directly by this scholarship, I can say with confidence he shared its constitutionalist, anti-rhetorical convictions.

Bush meant his presidency to be a criticism and correction of the rhetorical and other excesses of the "Reagan revolution." He meant to routinize or constitutionalize that revolution. He aimed to replace personal, rhetorical, and ideological leadership with good, meaning effective and relatively uncontroversial, government. He hoped to win reelection based upon his solid accomplishments, which would speak for themselves.

The Federalist's Anti-Leadership Presidency

President Bush seemed to follow *The Federalist* in hoping to reduce executive leadership largely to administration, to the perpetuation of the political forms established by others. He shared its antagonism to "leaders," defined by *The Federalist* as those who would impose their own forms or "vision" in place of the Constitution's. Ambitious leaders cannot help but attempt to arouse the people against given order and on behalf of their own.[2]

The Federalist's view of leaders is ambivalent. Their demagogic influence is beneficial when revolution is desirable. It is pernicious when it opposes good government. The Constitution, as good government, must oppose the influence of leadership. Bush believed that his time was one which could be particularly anti-revolutionary, because he was well positioned to provide an especially good form of constitutional government.

The Federalist regards good government as stable government. Unstable government, by threatening rights or person and property with revolution, is always bad government. A government which aids people effectively in securing their rights will always tend to be stable. What separated the extended, diverse republic created by the Constitution from previous democratic experiments is the likelihood of its long duration. The Constitution effectively freed democracy from its deserved bad reputation.

The Constitution, *The Federalist* says, strongly empowers the president so that he will be its partisan. The combination of a long fixed term with the possibility of indefinite reeligibilility allows and inspires him to pursue projects in the people's, the Constitution's, and his own long-term interests. He is given the power and incentive to oppose popular "inclinations," "temporary delusions" often inflamed by the "arts" of "flattering leaders" (*Federalist* 71).

The Federalist's president looks beyond the unstable whimsy of rhetorically aroused opinions to the people's more enduring gratitude. He hopes, in the best case, to have "lasting monuments" erected to his "courage and magnanimity" (*Federalist* 71). In President Bush's less lofty words, he hopes that his prudence and honor will win him a lasting place in history.

The president, more immediately, aims at reelection, which *The Federalist* holds he can deserve. The Constitution leads him to trust in the people's ability to make periodic judgments about their interests, while distrusting the more impulsive forms of public opinion. The people judge well when they reflect upon the results of policy. They judge badly on the basis of rhetorical appeals, which replace deliberation about interest with unreflective passion. The Constitution aims to lead people to judge deeds, not words.

The president will be able to use his constitutional power to protect himself from the destructiveness of leaders. They are most powerfully animated by an indiscriminate hatred of those in power. This hatred extends especially to the idea that the president might legitimately exercise his constitutional power. Leaders always aim to undermine the Constitution and executive firmness on its behalf.

The high probability that leaders will often succeed in temporarily misleading the people is one reason why executive firmness cannot be rooted reliably in public opinion. Such opinion cannot be counted on to give the president the energy he needs to govern effectively. Rhetorical leadership is usually more effective in opposition. Its legitimation, our time has shown, typically empowers the president's opponents more than the president himself. It is harder to defend plans and accomplishments in public debate than attack them. A time dominated by leaders is one in which the voters are easily and repeatedly moved by indignant campaigns "against Washington." President Bush did not share that hatred, and he believed he could minimize its influence. He believed his presidency would change to some extent the character of his time.

Recent presidents have tended to believe that they can and must govern as rhetorical leaders. The expectation has developed that they do so. They have become partisans of crisis. To find enough energy to govern, they attempt to arouse the people to an awareness of their critical situation.

Leadership, so understood, opposes the constitutional formalities which promote deliberation. It aims at the simple imposition of presidential will. But it has not really tended to strengthen the presidency. It has made the incumbent more vulnerable, because he is expected always to be extraordinary. People come to expect too much from the president and too much from government. They become too open to leaders' indiscriminate hatred or contempt for what government does. Incumbents have been too easily swept aside by the perception of crisis.

Bush's Bipartisan Constitutionalism

President Bush believed that the Reagan revolution could be stabilized, or protected from leadership, if it were purged of controversy. He aimed to achieve this goal in a time of "divided government," when the opposition promoted by the separation of powers is routinely inflamed by partisan animosity. Bush viewed divided government as promising a certain kind of stability through a mixture of the parties' overly contentious principles. Good government required both the president's and the Congress's constitutional acceptance of the legitimacy of that mixture.

Bush literally began his presidency by offering to make divided government good government. In his inaugural address, he called for "a new engagement . . . between the Executive and Congress." The time for "diviseness" and "dissension," rooted, he claimed, in the memory of Vietnam, must come to an end. The "old bipartisanship" that existed prior to that war "must begin anew again."

The new president reached out in friendship to the "loyal opposition" of Democratic congressional leaders. He envisioned their hard but friendly negotiations as aiming at good government, a strong foreign policy and a fiscally sound budget. The president said nothing about the principles— economic, cultural, or constitutional—that separated the parties. He said nothing moralistic that would inflame animosity.

This call for bipartisanship brought to mind the American foreign poli cy of the 1950s and early 1960s. Then there was general agreement between the branches and the parties concerning American purpose and strategy in the world. Divided government during the Eisenhower administration did not produce contentious foreign policy. Bush made it seem that all policy in the 1990s could be based on such bipartisanship. All that was necessary was to forget Vietnam, the now irrelevant cause of national division.

President Bush had no intention, even at the beginning, of repeating what he regarded as Reagan's error of wasting energy in futile battles with Congress over public opinion. He had no intention of attempting to impose his domestic agenda through rhetorical leadership. Instead, he designed a strategy to remove most domestic issues from controversy. He was especially interested in negotiating compromises on those issues which might be used by the Democrats to gain partisan advantage in public opinion. He sought the reputation for moderate activism on education, civil rights, the environment, and other contentious issues. He hoped to negotiate compromises that would produce a record of uncontroversial achievement. He wanted to restore *The Federalist*'s preference for policy made by coalition-building among a wide variety of interests, hoping that the process would mute ideological commitment and partisan animosity.[3]

President Bush also decided not to risk controversy by pushing for substantial budget cuts that would affect sizable constituencies. He called for cuts in general, knowing that the people in general would want them. But, for him, finding specific cuts was primarily the constitutional responsibility of Congress. The president said he wished for a balanced budget amendment and a line-item veto, but he surely did not wish for the contention that their actual existence would cause. He used their non-existence as an occasion for leadership or demagoguery, for explaining why he could not do what he was not inclined to do.

Bush believed that the contemporary expectation that the president pursue a legislative agenda through rhetorical leadership gives the president more policy-making responsibility than the Constitution ordinarily allows him to exercise effectively. This expectation is particularly unrealistic during a time of divided government, and for a president with at best quite ordinary rhetorical gifts. It readily leads to the perception of a failed presidency.

The president also believed that domestic strife and rhetorical leadership actually sap energy for the presidency. He aimed to save that energy to distinguish himself through the pursuit of foreign policy goals most Americans hold in common. His inclination was to prepare the presidency for the unexpected challenges that his foreign policy responsibilities would inevitably provide. He believed he could avoid domestic crises, but he was glad for the need to be ready for international ones. The latter sort of crisis, handled decisively and skillfully, could unite the nation without much need for rhetorical leadership. It would also prove Bush's worthiness to be president.

Bush's Use of Constitutional Power

Bush's decision to forego rhetorical leadership and pursue legislative compromise meant that he intended to govern with his constitutional powers alone.[4] He had an unusually fine understanding of those powers. He knew that the restoration of interbranch comity depended upon each branch knowing and respecting the nature and limits of its own power and the power of the other. The president had a far better appreciation than his immediate predecessors of the ways in which the separation of powers primarily empowers the executive to act independently and decisively. One reason he pursued a clear, constitutional definition of executive and legislative responsibilities is that he saw that their confusion had been at the expense of executive power and responsibility. He acted consistently to use his constitutional powers to protect them from legislative usurpation.

This reliance on constitutional powers is the core of *The Federalist*'s presidency. Bush's adroit use of them really did make him in some respects more energetic than Reagan. He was strikingly successful in establishing precedents that made the president's primacy in foreign policy more secure than before the Vietnam War. He did so largely by showing that *The Federalist* is right in holding that the president's perspective is the clearest view from which to make judgments concerning the nation's interests. Bush saw, for example, more clearly than anyone else what had to be done in the Gulf, made clear that he would do it, and through his decisive, effective action led Congress and the people to accept his judgment. He also led commentators to observe that presidential power, skillfully deployed, is more than sufficient to move a nation, and hence that rhetorical power had been overrated.

President Bush also arguably made better use of the veto than any of his predecessors. He knew, as *The Federalist* says, that the power of the veto exists primarily "to enable" the executive "to defend himself . . . against an immediate attack on his constitutional rights" (*Federalist* 75). Bush's uncharacteristically clear explanations of his self-defense vetoes are accounts of the president's rights and responsibilities under the Constitution.

Bush also used the credible threat of the veto as a way of negotiating with Congress over policy. Much more reliably than Reagan, he used the veto when Congress would not bargain, when it showed no inclination to alter legislation in ways the president could accept. His skillful use of the veto became a cause for wonder. He showed the extent to which the president could influence the character of legislation without resorting to popular appeals. For most of his term, Bush's policy vetoes were not a source of presidential unpopularity or perceived as a show of weakness (all defense, no offense). They were admired as evidence of the alleged wimp's unexpected strength.

The president used all this power to aim at winning by deserving reelection. This fact has been misinterpreted to mean that Bush would have done anything to keep his job. But the 1992 campaign showed that not to be the case. The president followed what he believed to be the best way to deserve reelection. He shared *The Federalist*'s view that the Constitution works best when an effective president is returned to office on the basis of the people's considered judgment about their interests. He hoped that his record would be solid enough that his critics on both the Left and the Right would seem merely quarrelsome, or out of touch with the facts. He would appear as a statesman; they would clearly be merely leaders.

Bush's goal was a "normal" election in 1992, one similar to the one which returned Eisenhower to office in 1956 or Coolidge in 1924. This election would also be like 1984 insofar as it would be an approval of the incumbent's strength of character as a condition for national and personal prosperity. Such a victory would not require the rhetorical excesses which Bush believed characterized Reagan's campaigns or his own in 1988. He hoped that there would be little "negative" about his campaign. He would depend on a largely nonpartisan evaluation of his character as reflected in his deeds. The extent of this nonpartisanship is seen in his assumption that the Democrats would continue to dominate Congress.

The Extent of Bush's Success

Bush's use of presidential power to secure a deserved second term seemed to work quite well for most of his term. His approval ratings were much more consistently high than Reagan's, and sometimes amazingly high. His critics complained with little effect that he succeeded in reducing what people expected from the president. Both liberals and conservatives argued that his administration lacked purpose or "vision." But this perception seemed not so much to be rejected as dismissed as unimportant by most Americans. Bush's merely but firmly constitutional administration seemed to fit the times. His possibilities, in any case, were limited by divided government. In domestic policy, he was only counted on to limit Congress's taxing and spending excesses, and to appoint anti-activist judges and bureaucrats.

The president's prudence seemed to serve him well in managing the end of the Cold War. But his popular approval actually neared unanimity with the wonderfully easy and overwhelming military victory in the Gulf. For a while, the president's deeds really did overwhelm his critics' words. One reason the Democratic ticket in 1992 was Clinton and Gore instead of

Cuomo and Nunn is that the first pair were not clearly on record as opposing the president's use of force in the Gulf.

Bush's foreign policy successes could reasonably be viewed as a stunning and rather unexpected vindication of the Reagan-Bush or firmly anticommunist approach to foreign policy. Both the victory in the Gulf, America's first substantial, unambiguous triumph on the battlefield in over four decades, and the disintegration of Soviet Communism owe much to the Reagan-led military buildup. The defeat of communism in Nicaragua, El Salvador, Afghanistan and elsewhere can also be attributed to often maligned but generally sound judgments of the Reagan administration. Under Bush, America achieved more completely than almost anyone dare imagine the strategic objectives of forty years of a foreign policy that realistically aimed only at communism's containment.

Bush's Vulnerability and His Failure
But this much more than solid success made President Bush far less invulnerable than his constitutional theory would suggest. Its result was to make Americans feel secure militarily, and so far less worried about international developments. Bush got almost all the vote from those who chose primarily on the basis of foreign policy in 1992, but they were less than 10% of the electorate. The Republican president suffered from the fact that 1992 was the first post-Cold War election.

Bush tried to make an election issue out of his foreign policy success. He said that victory was not inevitable, and that it was not really bi-partisan. It would not have occurred under a Democratic president, especially under the inexperienced, vacillating, and perhaps dishonorable Governor of Arkansas. Probably most Americans concurred with these judgments. But they seemed to add that now that victory had occurred, that America is militarily strong and safe, it is time to move on to the other sources of personal insecurity.

The president was influenced by advisors who believed that winning a war could win an election more than a year and a half later. They seemed ignorant of all American and modern, democratic experience. They also ignored readily discernible facts about human ingratitude and self-interest. The president may have been unlucky that the Cold War and the Gulf War ended as early as they did in his term. But he should have anticipated the results of these misfortunes much better than he did.

President Bush also had the misfortune of having the campaign take place in the midst of an unexpectedly prolonged recession. People ordinarily vote mainly on the basis of economic self-interest, and they to some large extent vote retrospectively. It is very difficult for an incumbent to be reelected when the economy is bad. The recession, of course, was global. With the exception of Britain's very lucky John Major, incumbents throughout the postindustrial world were defeated in 1992. Bush's theory of solid success assumed that the economy would not be bad during the election year, although he really could neither know nor control whether it would be or not.

But the portrayal of the president as the victim of a domestic misfortune beyond his control is misleading. For one thing, the voters, however unreasonably, held the president responsible, as *The Federalist* expected they would. For another, they seem to have perceived the economy as worse than it actually was. Almost no social scientist who predicts election outcomes with economic data thought Bush's defeat likely. But the voters' perception of this data, they should have known, can be more important than its reality.[5]

Clinton and Perot, both effective rhetorical leaders, greatly exaggerated the economy's problems. They said there was a crisis, "the worst economic mess since the Depression." They encouraged the people to feel their misery, and, because that was not enough, to fear for their future. They also led them to blame President Bush. Clinton and Perot cannot be blamed for their leadership. They did to Bush what Reagan did to Carter in 1980. But things were really worse in 1980, when interest rates and inflation were also extremely high. Why did Americans so readily believe Clinton and Perot? Why did their words overwhelm the effects of the incumbent's deeds, which easily could have been worse? Bush's electoral misfortune, contrary to his theory, was greater than he deserved.

When the voters judged Bush, they did not only do so retrospectively. They also looked to the future, to how they might be helped or hurt by a second Bush term. Their perception was that things "are on the wrong track," that the future would be worse than the present. That perception came not only from the president's critics, because he himself did not make it clear why things might get better. A view shared by many liberals and conservatives was that Bush's presidency was "spent," that there was no energy left for securing the nation's future.

Voters today are understandably more reluctant than *The Federalist* thought they would be to trust a president with a second term. Nixon's was a disaster. Reagan's was in many respects embarrassing when compared with the promise and performance of his first. Since the twenty-second amendment, which limits the president to two terms, second terms have characteristically been unenergetic and irresponsible. The second-term president cannot hope to complete long-terms projects. His opponents know they can wait him out. He is irresponsible in the sense that he knows that the voters cannot hold him accountable. The Constitution, in many ways, now becomes the president's enemy in his second term.

It is reasonable to ask how Bush would have performed without the incentive of reelection to organize and energize his administration. His *Federalist*-type theory would have lost its relevance. It is easy to see why voters would have more confidence in a first-term Clinton than a second-term Bush.

Voters were generally most concerned not with what Bush had done, but with what he would do. They looked for signals concerning his domestic policy, but they were confused. His theory did not allow him to see clearly why he would have to explain clearly what he would do. *The Federalist* says almost nothing about presidential campaigns, suggesting that incumbents ordinarily would not have to campaign. In this respect, its presidency is unrealistically nonpartisan and undemocratic. It does not accord with the experience of American elections, even before the rise of the rhetorical presidency.

The President's Revolutionary Leadership

The Federalist hoped that the Constitution would more completely supplant the revolution than it did. Substantial political controversy remained a characteristic feature of the American regime. Presidential elections have usually had a revolutionary component. They have been, in part, disputes concerning the continuing relevance of revolutionary principle under constitutional government. They have been arguments over liberty, equality, and democracy.

Presidential elections have been as much about progress as political stability. The Constitution has not impeded but, properly understood, secured the conditions for American progress. The energy given to the presidency from electoral victories, as well as energy supplied by the presidents personally, have been the chief engine of that progress. Presidential power, Bush did not see clearly enough, is necessarily dynamic and moral.

Successful American presidents have usually made it clear how their administrations have and will be informed by progressive principle. Because presidential elections have been democratic, progress must be toward democracy. There is no way simply to routinize or constitutionalize this continuation of revolutionary aspiration.

President Bush never did understand that he was elected not to stabilize or depoliticize but to continue the Reagan revolution. What that revolution aimed to do was to undo what Presidents Roosevelt and Johnson had accomplished during their Democratic revolutions. For the Democrats, progress toward democracy and prosperity depended upon equality and security increasingly being guaranteed by government. They spoke of a process by which government would become progressively more responsible for the solution of human problems, making human existence more just or equal. This process was also presented as a movement toward liberty, or freedom from the fear and anxiety that distort human individuality.

Part of Reagan's power as president was his successful identification of American progress with the "conservative" criticism of this Democratic liberalism. The Democratic movement, he said, was, in truth, toward equality in dependency and away from individual opportunity. It was also away from personal responsibility and toward the impersonal irresponsibility of bureaucratic regulation. It was toward the rule of a paternalistic elite composed of bureaucrats, judges, and intellectuals.

According to Reagan, material and moral progress both depend upon the individual securing his prosperity and dignity independently of big, impersonal government. The individual comes into his own in the context of communities such as the family, neighborhood, church, and local government, where the rule of personal responsibility is possible. Reagan made it seem that the reactionaries in America were not the conservatives who dominated his administration, but the liberals in Congress who would perpetuate and extend government dependency or entitlement in a time when freedom is progressing throughout the world. He called for progress through the restoration of the Constitution's original understanding of equality in liberty.

Reagan's policies, in his own mind, were always guided by this controversial articulation of constitutional principle.[6] He used the power of the presidency, broadly speaking, to deregulate. Employing rhetorical leadership, he sought and received a tax cut from Congress. He also sought, but did not really expect, corresponding budget cuts. Before Reagan, "responsible" Republicans mainly worried like accountants, thinking that spending must be cut before taxes. Reagan saw that the beginning of progress must be tax cuts and tax reform.

Progress must be away from government-sponsored redistribution and entitlement. Reagan's policy was that taxes should be cut for everyone, a democratic principle. The result, combined with no great domestic cuts and the cost of the military buildup, was to increase the deficit. But the newly large deficit was not all bad. It made bigger government seem impossible. Progress became possible only on Reagan's, and not the Democrats', terms.[7]

Reagan knew that the existence of divided government meant that people only half- or half-heartedly accepted his view of progress. They tended to want the Republicans' low taxes and the Democrats' high entitlements. They did not really mind that this mixture of principles is particularly irresponsible. But Reagan refused to accept the view of some Republicans and the Democrats that higher taxes could ever be responsible. He hoped that eventually the people could be brought by leadership or a genuine crisis to choose against entitlements.

President Reagan, contrary to his critics, also generally pursued in principle and policy social or cultural deregulation. He opposed bureaucratic and judicial intrusion upon personal and family responsibility. He used his power to appoint anti-activist judges, who sought to undo the Court's anti-democratic paternalism. Their purpose was to reverse *Roe v. Wade*, not because of their personal views on abortion but because the Constitution does not require or allow the Court to resolve the abortion controversy.

President Bush and the Reagan Revolution
In the 1988 campaign, Bush seemed to say enough to make clear that he would continue the Reagan revolution. His emphasis was on continuity and loyalty to the president. He also pledged unambiguously not to raise

taxes, and he showed his contempt for the cultural liberalism or elitism of his opponent.

But, as president, Bush did not make it clear enough whether he remained true either to Reagan's constitutional principles or his policies. In 1990, for example, he seemed to say he had come to believe that a large deficit was a greater evil than higher taxes. Negotiation and compromise with Congress, guided by this perception, led him to break his anti-tax pledge. To his credit, he departed from his anti-rhetorical precedents and attempted to explain to the American people why he had broken his promise. His explanation included hardly any opposition to Congress in principle or policy. He was followed on television by the Democratic Senator Mitchell, who also broke with recent custom to agree with the president in the name of good government. The budget agreement seemed a perfect example of the bipartisan process Bush hoped to establish.[8]

The president said a bipartisan agreement could bring the deficit under control and its rejection would bring recession. The recession came anyway. The deficit continued to increase rapidly. The president, not Congress, got most of the blame for both. He quickly repudiated the agreement, refusing to take responsibility for what he had done and confusing the voters even more.

Bush's aim to create a bipartisan or "good government" approach to the deficit problem led to the worst political mistake of his administration. Probably only the indifference to principle that is the precondition for this bipartisanship could have convinced the president that he and the Democratic congressional leaders could really agree to reduce the deficit. He should have known that any such agreement would mainly focus the contempt the people have for government's irresponsibility—even if it is largely a reflection of their own irresponsibility—on the president. He was counted on to follow Reagan's lead in firmly and publicly resisting Congress.

Bush's new position that the main economic worry is the deficit and his irresolution about taxes probably combined to reduce Americans' long-term confidence about their economy. This combination certainly made the president look more unprincipled than he really was. It made him vulnerable to the charge that the deficit was the creation or the responsibility of the Reagan-Bush presidency or of divided government ("gridlock").

It made it seem less the particular responsibility of the Democratic Congress.

The deficit, according to the president's critics, was the main cause of America's economic decline or lack of competitiveness. It caused not only the recession, but a broader and more critical economic malaise. The focus on the deficit, always avoided by Reagan but prepared for 1992 by Bush, leads people to doubt what prosperity they do enjoy. They believe that the economy is not performing as well as it seems. This uneasiness, of course, empowers opposition leaders.

Perot masterfully used this uneasiness to wean prosperous conservatives away from the president. He said that the economic crisis could only be resolved by a *de facto* suspension of the ordinary operation of the separation of powers. For him, gridlock did not mean divided government but constitutional separation. Perot flattered the American people almost beyond belief. He suggested that a simple majority would willingly accept the combination of severe budget cuts and higher taxes that he said was required to bring the deficit under control.

The demagogue Perot sounded dangerous, but he was not. He naively believed that the president, through rhetorical leadership, could become much more powerful than he is really permitted to be under the Constitution. His impressive vote came partly from those apolitical Americans most easily seduced by simple or demagogic solutions. But it also came from those who really believed that the deficit was the nation's major problem. This belief should not have produced a vote for Perot. Comparative analysis shows that the separation of powers, by distancing government some from the people's inclinations, actually retards deficit growth.[9] Bush missed this and many other rhetorical opportunities for a defense of American constitutionalism.

Clinton had the only plausible proposal for ending gridlock. A Democratic president must be elected to go with the inevitably Democratic Congress. But as a means for deficit reduction this proposal was plausible only if one does not believe that the Democratic Congress has been the deficit's main cause. To make divided government seem preferable, the Republican president repeatedly and effectively has to make the case against Congress. The budget agreement, based on Bush's nonpartisan constitutionalism, undermined fatally his ability to make that case. He allowed the argument to prevail that divided government is the enemy of progress.

To defend divided government, the president had to continue the Reagan revolution, employing its sometimes confrontational tactics and aggressive rhetoric. He should have publicly confronted Congress in 1990 and 1992. He should have said clearly and often that tax increases do not have a history of reducing deficits. By stifling economic growth and providing the means for more government spending, they in the long run increase them. By seeming to conspire with Democratic leaders to allow a record tax increase in 1990, Bush could not call credibly for a tax cut to get the country moving again in 1992. Nor could he credibly blame the recession on excessive taxing and spending.

Because he passed up these opportunities for rhetorical leadership, the president was accused effectively by opposition leaders of being insensitive to the suffering and insecurity produced by the recession. He really believed, and with good reason, that there was nothing much he could do to bring the recession to an end. On the level of actual policy, Bush did not panic. He was served well by his inclination to believe that government intervention usually makes things worse.

But, stung by the charge of insensitivity, the president was reduced during the campaign to promising Democratic-style programs and gimmicks. This demagoguery was ineffective because it was obviously unprincipled. Clinton and Perot had no trouble calling attention to the mere expediency of these last-minute ideas, as well as to their tacit admission of failure. They certainly did not characterize the president's administration as a whole. (The same sort of analysis applies to the leader-aroused perception of a health care crisis.)

Bush's rhetorical leadership on behalf of the continuation of the Reagan revolution would have been less demagogic than his attempt to campaign without relying on that leadership. His ineffective demagoguery seemed to come from his conviction that all rhetorical appeals are equally unworthy. He also seemed to see little connection between campaign rhetoric and the requirements of governing. He might have been reelected, and even had a successful second term, had he made his principles clear, as well as the connection between them and his policies. Unfortunately, where Reagan was strongest, Bush was weakest.

Clinton actually learned more about revolutionary leadership under the Constitution from Reagan than did Bush.[10] He spoke generally of change, and followed Reagan in making opportunity and responsibility the principles on which Americans should rest their hopes for a better tomorrow. He did not speak as a Democratic reactionary, a defender of discredited entitlements. He always sounded more progressive and often more like a Reaganite than the president.

Clinton's shrewd, Democratic addition to Reagan's principles was that Reagan and Bush did not really believe in them. He portrayed them as economic elitists who believe that low taxes and deregulation for the rich would benefit all. Clinton promised really to extend the benefits of Reaganism to all.

Bush was easy prey for this leadership because he did not give the democratic argument for the economic liberty favored by Republicans. He did not explain why the free market does not primarily benefit, as Clinton charged, his rich friends. He did not even begin to defend Reagan from the tired charge that his policy was "trickle down." What the part of the world emerging out of the rubble of communism had discovered about the interdependence of democracy and liberty the American, Republican president seemed not to know.

Culture and Quayle

There were other issues besides economic ones in 1992, and on each of them Bush was less vulnerable. The campaigned focused on the economy, as Clinton intended, mostly because Bush was ineffective in raising other issues. I have already considered foreign policy. Much more promising were the "family values" issues, especially when connected to what Vice President Quayle called "cultural elitism."

Bush used these issues to good effect to discredit his opponent in 1988. Differences in style and better campaign management made Clinton a more elusive target than Dukakis, but his genuine positions on the social or cultural issues were probably no less vulnerable. When the president was charged early in the campaign with diversion and demagoguery for raising these issues, he almost completely dropped them. He did so because he seemed not to believe in them. It was not clearly his view that the deterioration of personal and parental responsibility can be traced to bureaucratic regulation and judicial fiat. He also seemed not to see that the decay of the conditions that make possible parental responsibility affect especially the lives of ordinary and disadvantaged Americans. Again, Bush did not follow Reagan in giving the democratic argument for his principles and policy.

Actually, the president's policies in resisting cultural deterioration had been fairly steadfast. He could have taken some pride, for example, in his anti-activist judicial appointments. But, because he did not defend his position in a principled, democratic way, he left the rhetorical field to the leadership of his opponents. The "media" soundly defeated him, as it never did Reagan, only because he did not effectively engage them. He seemed to have believed the media elite when it reported that the Republican cultural positions are somehow both unpopular and vulgar, and that the constitutional arguments on their behalf are outside the respectable mainstream of constitutional discourse.

Yet despite almost everything one reads and hears, the fact is that even a majority of those who voted with abortion (the most contentious and problematic of the cultural issues) in mind voted for the president. What if the president could have actually explained the relationship between his policies and "family values"? What if these explanations had compelled Clinton actually to make clear and defend the Democratic positions on these policies? Bush seemed to believe he could win without arousing cultural or moral animosity. But Clinton's talented advisors, who said "the economy, stupid," believed that only such animosity might reelect the president.

Quayle made a spirited effort to confront the media on the cultural issues. He failed not because his positions were wrong or unpopular,[11] but because he is inarticulate and not very intelligent. He, like the president, experienced exceptional difficulty in presenting coherent explanations, although he seemed to have a greater interest in doing so.

An important presidential power, by party custom, is the selection of his running mate. Bush chose badly in 1988, although he had plenty of time. The intelligence and rhetorical abilities of his choice seemed to be of no interest to him. Yet the vice president might have supplied what he himself lacked. The choice of Quayle must be evidence of the extent to which Bush believed he could govern effectively without rhetorical leadership. His critics, with good reason, said it confirmed the contempt for *logos* they already discerned the president's own speech.

The magnitude of this careless miscalculation was large, if difficult to measure. A respectable running mate, polls show, would have given Bush a landslide in 1988. The cumulative effect on the administration's reputation of the innumerable jokes, articles, and even books based on Bush's and Quayle's verbal gaffes must have had a significant effect in 1992. Many of the criticisms, of course, were unfair. But many serious citizens, both liberal and conservative, were embarrassed and repulsed by the "bully pulpit" having become the "silly pulpit." Refined cultural conservatives were distressed by the way Quayle's leadership discredited their positions. The comparison of Bush and Quayle with the glib Clinton and Gore was striking. The Democrats were able to give quick, detailed, plausible, and often edifying explanations about every issue under the sun. They were so much more articulate that many voters came to believe that they must be more competent.

Conclusion: Bush's Impossible Conservatism

President Bush believed he could resist the tendency of his rhetorical, anti-constitutional time by winning reelection without resorting much to rhetorical leadership. But his deeds did not overwhelm his opponents' words. They were still able to create a perception of crisis. In dealing with such perception, the president, because he was inarticulate, seemed incompetent.

Bush seemed to believe that, for him, a successful presidency would not be hard, and most commentators agreed with him for most of his term. But all American experience, not just that in our, rhetorical time, pointed to his failure. Walter Dean Burnham has shown that presidents elected as "promising conservators of the 'revolution' carried out by others" seem always to fail. Such "regime conservators" are never good at providing policy visions of their own or "positive, sustained leadership in dealing with the country's problems."[12] Their conservatism is always too constitutional or not revolutionary enough. Even under the Constitution, too extreme an attachment to regime conservation leads to defeat by those who aim at "change," or regime transformation. Presidential leadership is always required for presidents to resist leadership effectively.

Notes

1. See, for example, Jeffrey K. Tulis, *The Rhetorical Presidency* (Princeton: Princeton University Press, 1987) and James Ceaser, *Presidential Selection: Theory and Development* (Princeton: Princeton University Press, 1979).

2. *The Federalist*'s view of leaders is presented in greater detail in my "*The Federalist*'s Hostility to Leadership and the Crisis of the Contemporary Presidency," *Presidential Studies Quarterly* 17 (Fall 1987): 711–24.

3. On Bush's strategy, see Michael Duffy and Dan Goodgame, *Marching in Place: The Status Quo Presidency of George Bush* (New York: Simon and Schuster, 1992). See especially pp. 58–62. All I do is give a more friendly or less muckraking view of the information they present. I also found the chapter, "Making the Process Work: The Procedural Presidency of George Bush," in Aaron Wildavsky's *The Beleaguered Presidency* (New Brunswick, N.J.: Transaction, 1991), pp. 301–52, quite useful in pointing the way to Bush's constitutional conservatism.

4. I am greatly indebted to the analysis and information concerning Bush's understanding and use of presidential power in Terry Eastland, *Energy in the Executive: The Case for the Strong Presidency* (New York: Free Press, 1992).

5. See James Ceaser and Andrew Busch, *Upside Down and Inside Out: The 1992 Election and American Politics* (Lanham, MD: Littlefield Adams Quality Paperbacks, 1993), pp. 35–6, 53, note 8. Also, Seymour Martin Lipset, "The Significance of the 1992 Election," *PS: Political Science and Politics* 26 (March 1993): 7–16.

6. See William K. Muir, *The Bully Pulpit: The Presidential Leadership of Ronald Reagan* (San Francisco: Institute for Contemporary Studies Press, 1992).

7. See Wildavsky, pp. 213–40. Compare with the analysis of Reagan's strategy in Harvey C. Mansfield Jr., *America's Constitutional Soul* (Baltimore: Johns Hopkins University Press, 1991).

8. See Eastland, pp. 49–63.

9. See James Q. Wilson, "Does the Separation of Powers Still Work?" in Robert E. DiClerico, ed., *Analyzing the Presidency*, 2nd ed. (Guilford, CT: Duskin Publishing, 1990), p. 105.

10. On the superiority of Clinton's rhetoric and explanations, see Harvey C. Mansfield, Jr., "Change and Bill Clinton," *Times Literary Supplement*, November 13, 1992, pp. 14–15.

11. See Barbara Dafoe Whitehead, "Dan Quayle Was Right," *The Atlantic Monthly* 271 (April 1993): 47–83.

12. Walter Dean Burnham, "The Legacy of George Bush: Travails of an Understudy," Gerald M. Pomper, ed., *The Election of 1992: Reports and Interpretations* (Chatham, N.J.: Chatham House, 1992), p. 2.

10

In Search of American Conservatism

This is clearly a conservative moment in American political life, although only fools predict how long such a moment might last. Conservative Republicans control Congress and the American political agenda, and experts speculate about the possible disappearance of the liberal Democratic Party altogether.

President Clinton will probably win another term. That is partly because he is posing as a conservative, signing, for example, the Republicans' welfare reform measure. It is also partly because the economy seems strong and the nation is at peace. But it is mostly because the Republican nominee, Bob Dole, seems incapable of mobilizing a conservative majority coalition.

This is more clearly a conservative moment in American political thought. Conservatives remain an embattled minority in American intellectual life, but political ideas they have. Their opponents, the liberals, radicals, and postmodernists, seem intellectually exhausted, with nothing new or even timely to say. Hopes for radical transformation or liberation are passé. Socialism died in 1989, and the new American consensus is that the most powerful effect of the social revolution of the 1960s has been the growth of personal irresponsibility. The liberals have become the reactionaries. They defend, against the grain of public opinion and with discredited arguments, privileges they secured from Congress when they ruled.

The distinction between liberalism and conservatism present in America today originated with the respected professor of philosophy John Dewey's redefinition of liberalism as no longer freedom from government but freedom through government-sponsored social action in the early 1930s. President Franklin Roosevelt, in his attempt to purify his welfare-state Democratic Party in 1938, said that America is now divided politically into two "schools of thought." The liberal school holds that the development of the welfare state, the growth in the use of the cooperative efforts of government to solve human problems, constitutes human progress. The conservative school holds that the institutions of the welfare state are undesirable and unnecessary. The problems of modern life are still best addressed through personal initiative and private philanthropy.

On Roosevelt's terms, it is almost impossible to be a liberal in America today. Only a few Democratic members of Congress, and certainly not President Clinton, believe in the possibility or goodness of the further expansion of the welfare state. The huge government deficit and funding crises in basic programs such as Social Security and Medicare make it difficult enough to imagine sustaining what already exists over the long term. Clinton's abandoned attempt at liberalism was his plan for government funding of health care, in imitation of Canadian and European social democracies. But the plan floundered over the issue of funding and the voters' distrust of government in general.

Techno-Optimism and Libertarianism

Today's conservatives, with few exceptions, do not favor the complete dismantling of the welfare state. But they do oppose Roosevelt's liberalism on what constitutes human progress. The development of the welfare state has largely been a period of decline, of a growth in dependency and irresponsibility. Genuine progress liberates the individual from all forms of dependence for self-sufficiency and personal fulfillment. The scope of liberation has the promise of becoming unprecedented in view of the amazing possibilities of contemporary technology.

This conservative, progressive optimism is at the heart of the famous futurology of the Speaker of the House, Newt Gingrich, the most powerful and capable political leader in America today. It is also present in the rhetoric of "empowerment" of former Congressman and Cabinet member and current vice presidential nominee, Jack Kemp. This optimism originated with the "supply side" economists who gave the Reagan Administration its distinctive vision, such as Jude Wanniski and Paul Craig Roberts. Their spokespersons among the 1996 presidential contenders were Senator Phil Gramm and millionaire publisher Steve Forbes. The appeal of Forbes' cheerful message that a change in the tax law, by itself, can produce a wide array of beneficial social consequences was surprising. Gramm's campaign floundered because his abrasive personality and annoying voice negate the optimism of his words.

Techno-optimism now dominates what is called the libertarian wing of American conservatism, the radical form of anti-statist individualism that first captured the hearts of many Republicans with the presidential candidacy of Barry Goldwater in 1964. But even for Americans to call libertarianism conservatism is confusing. Libertarianism, after all, is really nineteenth century *laissez faire* liberalism, including the tendency toward anarchist utopianism. Its premise is that human beings flourish best free from the constraints not only of government but even of tradition and custom. It tends to be not only antipolitical but asocial, and it is conservative only in the negative sense of opposing welfare-state liberalism.

Libertarianism is invariably elitism. Its view of liberty is contrary to the experience of most human beings, who see liberty as good only when constrained by stable institutions. Libertarian tenets became temporarily popular as part of the resentment of "angry white males" against redistributive government programs such as welfare and affirmative action. But this anger is not directed against all government programs, certainly not against those, such as Medicare, from which white males benefit and upon which they have become accustomed to depend. Pure libertarianism will never become populism or majoritarianism.

Cultural Conservatism

For conservatism to have become majoritarianism in America, it had to embrace more than "negative freedom." The populist form of conservatism is social or cultural, or not primarily economic. The libertarians are actually social or cultural liberals, joining the Democrats in being pro-choice or permissive when it comes to abortion, pornography, divorce, religion, sexual orientation, and so forth. The state governor perhaps most devoted to deregulation and economic freedom, libertarian Republican William Weld of Massachusetts, is also the one with the most extremely permissive view of abortion and gay rights.

Social or cultural conservatives oppose liberalism's tendency to lapse into moral relativism with moral traditionalism and religion. Such conservatives criticize the pernicious consequences of "secular humanism" on public policy, its contribution to the decline of the family and the growth of personal irresponsibility. They also criticize the elitism of cultural liberalism, showing both its contempt for and its reduction in the quality of the lives of most ordinary, decent, religious Americans. Perhaps the leading cultural conservative today is former Secretary of Education William Bennett, who has written best-sellers on indicators of moral decline, the intellectual movement responsible for America's demoralization, and two on the use of edifying literature to restore the teaching of virtue.

The cultural conservatives join the libertarians in their opposition to much government regulation of the economy, because such regulation is used to impose secularism, and in their suspicion of the professionally-trained and intellectually fashionable experts who shape the policy of the national government. But the libertarians would join the liberals in using the power of the Courts to check state and local government's tendency often to be friendly to religion, enact moral regulations, and discourage abortion. The cultural conservatives would use state and local government as an agent of morality, and they expect the president and Congress to use their power to curb meddlesome judges and bureaucrats. The gap that separates the libertarians from the cultural conservatives here is wide. The pro-life movement became a political force in America as a result of a Supreme Court decision, *Roe v. Wade*, which invalidated the laws of almost all the states substantially restricting abortion.

Culturally conservative thought exists in varying degrees of intensity. There is a religious revival in America today, and its heart is evangelical and fundamentalist Protestantism. Two striking, if not completely unprecedented, features of this revival are the large amount of political activity it has generated and its insistence that Biblical principles inform all of one's life. As Alexis de Tocqueville first noted in the 1830s, American Christianity, most of the time, has been distinguished by clergy distancing themselves from political life. They have tacitly conceded that the worlds of politics and business will be mostly secular and liberal. They have not expected wholehearted religious devotion from most American believers. The reasonable goal of American clergy has been only to limit the restless materialism and anxious disorientation produced by modern liberty and the dogma of equality.

Conservative Christians (including some but not yet a great number of Catholics) are now politically organized as the "Christian Coalition," which played a large role in the recent Republican takeover of Congress. This organization is both well-disciplined and populist. It is capable of mobilizing more than one-third of the Republican primary vote in many of the states, and it controls the party organization in half or more of them.

If its support is not quite indispensable, its hostility was thought to be fatal for Republican presidential candidates in 1996.

The political agenda of the "religious right" goes beyond curbing big government's hostility to religion and enacting pro-life legislation. Its larger goal is to restore what it holds to be America's original self-understanding as a Christian nation. Its authors zealously, if quite questionably, endeavor to show the Christian inspiration of the American founders.

The conservative authors of the religious revival are almost completely unknown to most American intellectuals and are absent from the mainstream media. Their books go unreviewed in the secular press, and they do not show up on *The New York Times* best-seller list, which is based upon a survey of secular bookstores. But many of them have huge sales through Christian bookstores, particularly, but not only, in the Midwest, South, and West.

The exception to this anonymity are the strange books of the televangelist and former presidential candidate Pat Robertson, whose empire includes a university with an accredited law school. Robertson's books are full of conspiracy theorizing that depends to some extent on antisemitism, and they are easy targets for the liberal media. Conservative Jews, such as *Commentary*'s Norman Podhoretz, rushed to Robertson's defense, citing his resolute support for Israel. They did not dwell on the apocalyptic Biblical interpretation on which that support is based. But Robertson's books are not typical of a body of literature that is far more pious than paranoid.

More remarkable than political activism or the flourishing, almost covert, intellectual life is the surge in popularity of new groups promoting the self-discipline of a wholly Christian way of life. One of these, Promise Keepers, is for men only. It inspires and trains them to become responsible, devoted heads of the families as the Bible teaches, opposing the selfish individualism and cultural permissiveness that, by liberating men from their duties, have torn the family apart. Literally more than a million of American men have gathered at Promise Keeper rallies in football stadiums, and fittingly their founder and leader is a former University of Colorado football coach. Another sign of this new Christian self-discipline is the rapid growth in the number of Americans "home schooling" their children, usually because they have devoted themselves to raising their children as Christians and fear the corrupting secularism of public education.

For astute sociologists such as James Davison Hunter, the rise of the religious right is evidence of a "culture war" in America today. The cultural conservatives organized defensively at first, but they are now on offensive, hoping to transform the nation. A moderate observer, following Hunter's lead, might say that the Democratic Party has become too secular and permissive, the Republican Party too religiously or culturally conservative, and that most Americans stand somewhere in the middle. Certainly the longing for moderation was one source for the wide early support for General Colin Powell's aborted presidential bid. But a cultural conservative would respond with data that show that most Americans are somewhat religious in a rather orthodox way, concerned and anxious about moral decline, and favor some conservative reform to address that decline. Certainly a religiously-based, populist, cultural conservatism is what distinguishes America from the other nations of the West today. As Tocqueville said, the Americans are singular in their confidence in the interdependence of the spirit of religion and the spirit of liberty.

Traditionalism
Well before the religious revival, Russell Kirk, through the publication of *The Conservative Mind* (1953), founded modern American conservatism. For Kirk, conservatism is Burkean traditionalism, or grateful veneration for the good life made possible through established order. Kirk believed himself to be in the tradition of the conservatism that came into existence in Europe in opposition to the spirit of the French Revolution, but also part of the millennium-long Anglo-Saxon tradition of prescriptive rights and the rule of law and, more comprehensively still, part of the longer Western tradition of adherence to natural and divine law. Kirk opposed abstract reason with concrete experience, appeals to liberated nature with tradition and natural law, universal rights with particular duties, and the idea of man's indefinite perfectibility with the truth about his sinful and otherwise limited existence under God.

Kirk claimed that America had its own conservative tradition, but his case depends upon rejecting a good part of the American tradition. Arguably all American political disputes center on disputes concerning the meaning of the principles set forth in Thomas Jefferson's revolutionary document, the Declaration of Independence. But for Kirk, the Declaration was partly an American aberration (Jefferson's was no conservative mind) and partly merely a statement of separation, not revolution, with no enduring significance. The genuinely American constitutional principles, the rule of law, the protection of property, and so forth, are all inheritances from the English constitutional tradition. For this conclusion, Kirk can find some support in Tocqueville, who says the idea of rights is beautiful, not useful, and so aristocratic, not Lockean. But Tocqueville meant to present a muted criticism of the American founders' self-understanding, and I think Kirk does too. Kirk's conservatism, paradoxically, is innovative, an effort to improve on the American foundation in view of its weaknesses.

The best American traditionalist political statement is Wilmoore Kendall and George Carey's *The Basic Symbols of the American Political Tradition* (1970). They claim the connection usually made between the Declaration and the Constitution was Abraham Lincoln's "derailment" of traditional principle caused by revolutionary, messianic fervor. They take the Confederate side in the Civil War, holding that the Southern understanding of the American tradition is the best and the truest one. Their stand tends to be anti-technological or anti-modern, and so in today's context rather anti-Newt (Gingrich). It finds its origin in the Agrarian Movement of Southern intellectuals in the 1930s.

This Confederate conservatism reached its highest level of literary refinement and erudition in the writing of M.E. Bradford, who attempted to recover the love of Christian and classical virtue, tradition, and place he found in some of the founders and in the old South. Despite their beauty, Bradford's books remain somewhat outside even the conservative mainstream, because of his unapologetic attitude toward the South's racially-based slavery and segregation, and because of his extreme attack on Lincoln, perhaps America's most celebrated political hero, for his "gnostic" rhetoric. Tocqueville noted that the only genuine aristocrats in America were the Southern masters, and their cultivated world lives on in the imaginations of a few literary figures today. The traditionalists, by taking a rebel's stand, tend toward romanticism. But perhaps they do well to rebel against the materialism, vulgarity, and mediocrity that characterize high-tech democracy. Traditionalists were most attracted to the combination of rebel nationalism and aggressive moral revivalism of Pat Buchanan's presidential campaign. Some seem pleased that Buchanan's cause imitates theirs in being right, and so lost, from the beginning.

The conservative, traditionalist followers of Kirk, who have some if far from the dominant influence in the Republican Party, are now called paleoconservatives. The traditionalists have embraced this journalistic label with rebellious pride. It suggests that they are actually reactionaries, or devoted to a way of life that cannot be revived. It also suggests the truth of what they whine: they are an oppressed minority even in the conservative movement today. Their most angry apologist, Paul Gottfried, has documented in extensive detail the fact that most of the conservative foundation money goes to those the paleos say are not conservative at all.

Neoconservatism

The paleos say, with some reason, that the conservatives, to become intellectually respectable, had to become liberals. In the intellectual world at least, the dominant group of conservatives today is called neoconservative. The neoconservatives are newly conservative; they used to be liberal. They sometimes say they have changed sides largely in response to changed circumstances, not because they have changed their principles.

The first generation of neos typically began as socialists in the 1930s, matured into welfare state liberals, began to express conservative doubts about liberalism, became Reaganites, and finally Republicans. The neos were born in and find themselves at home in cities, mostly in New York but more recently in Washington. They are urbane, well-educated, and well-connected. They are often Jewish, although not often observant, sometimes Catholic, and most rarely Protestant. They have no experience with, interest in, or affection for the agrarian, Protestant, small-town, somewhat traditionalist life of the American nineteenth century. The most distinguished and profound of the neos is Irving Kristol.

Kristol came to see that liberal democracy depends on certain cultural preconditions that are themselves somewhat illiberal, and his concern became protecting what is required for the perpetuation of human, and so limited, liberty. He became a conservative liberal, and so he opposes traditionalism insofar as it has unnecessarily illiberal implications, or promotes racism, religious tyranny, meddlesome moralism, and so forth. He views the neos as in sympathetic alliance, not complete agreement, with the religious right. The measured, mixed character of Kristol's judgments is also present in his famous decision to give capitalism "two cheers." He praises it for its production of wealth and so comfortable self-preservation for more people than ever before, its role in protecting all forms of liberty, and its promotion of personal responsibility. But he withholds the third cheer in view of the vulgarity of its utilitarianism, its lack of appreciation for the intrinsic splendor of virtue, and he recommends that we turn to the premodern philosophers and theologians for such an appreciation.

Kristol criticizes the libertarians for their neglect of the formation of character or virtue, while agreeing with much of their economic analysis. He agrees with the traditionalists that the decency of capitalist society depends on its precapitalistic or traditional inheritances, which economic and technological progress does tend to erode. So the neoconservatives think the techno-optimism of Speaker Gingrich and others is naive. No form of technical progress can ever resolve the moral questions which human beings must answer to live responsibly, and unfettered technological development is morally destructive. This neoconservative subtlety is not clearly mirrored in Dole's presidential campaign, and they seem to have written him off as a lost cause.

The Straussians

The tone and concerns of his writing, not to mention his own acknowledgment of debts in his autobiographical reflections, make it clear that Kristol's thought has been decisively shaped by the work of Leo Strauss. Strauss, a German Jewish emigré to America in the 1930s, has had an extensive and profound influence on American conservative thought as a whole. He followed suggestions found in the writing of both Martin Heidegger and Moses Maimonides to recover the lost, esoteric horizon of the classical political philosophy of Plato, Aristotle, and Xenophon, the original justification of the mixture of liberty and authority, or philosophy, politics, and theology, that has characterized the West in its vitality.

Strauss's seductive, breathtaking presentation of the classical perspective has formed thousands of American scholars, as many of whom have worked for the government as in the universities. The outstanding "Straussian" in political life today is William Kristol (Ph.D., Harvard, a student of the most witty and erudite of the Straussians, Harvey C. Mansfield, Jr.), Irving's son, Republican master strategist and founder of the new, instantly famous, and universally read conservative magazine, *The*

Weekly Standard. The younger Kristol earned his reputation as a political genius by successfully urging Senator Dole to oppose the president completely on national heath care, when all the other experts counseled compromise.

Strauss's thought combined theoretical radicalism with practical conservatism, avoiding the traditionalist's hostility to reason and the liberal's or the technocrat's naive utopianism. He urged his students to defend America's liberal democracy, not as a Lockean or modern or liberal project, but as the best possible regime for the future of philosophic or liberated inquiry. He said the philosophers will always be few, and the many, at best, will be formed by the prudent deceptions of sound law and tradition. It is both the duty and in the self-interest of the few to protect the many from the morally corrosive and debilitating effects of excessive Enlightenment. By allowing so many of his students to believe that they shared the intellectual liberation of a very rare few, Strauss gave them an incentive to exercise practical responsibility, to be politically conservative. They take pride in their conservatism, evidence as it is that they are wiser than their fellow intellectuals.

The students of Strauss are a large and contentious enough group to have divided into identifiable conservative factions, two of which are particularly easy to identify. One faction, followers of Harry Jaffa, teaches that the American founding, articulated through a close, discerning, Lincolnian reading of the Declaration of Independence, is a perfect embodiment of the natural law/natural rights tradition inaugurated by the classical political philosophers. The Jaffaites turn on anyone who criticizes or misinterprets the founding. It is difficult to tell whether their partisanship is genuinely philosophical or merely moral, a spirited defense of one's own.

Other students of Strauss follow Allan Bloom and Thomas Pangle. They more openly and aggressively teach the incoherence of all morality, including America's own, and they proclaim the certain superiority of the liberated rationalism of the philosophic life. In his Straussian best-seller, *The Closing of the American Mind,* Bloom defends morality for the sake of philosophy. He says that American students, influenced too early by popularized philosophic currents, come to the university too morally relativistic to take anything seriously, even Socrates or Bloom. Their excessive openness has closed them to the possibility of wisdom.

Bloom's book was initially well-received by conservatives because of its penetrating, unfashionable criticism of easygoing, "nice" relativism. But they soon noticed that Bloom never calls himself a conservative, and that he found almost nothing about American moral and political life worth conserving. Conservatives also complained about Bloom's hostility to religion. That complaint is also brought against Strauss himself. He says reason cannot refute the claims of revelation, but he seems rather definitely to take the side of reason against revelation. Also noticed has been Strauss's hostility to Christianity. He seems to judge modern philosophers as philosophers, in part, by their certainty that Christianity could not possibly be true. But, as Bloom says, Strauss did see that the Bible must be read with the attitude of a potential believer, and Strauss did seem to do so. There is no evidence that Bloom ever did. A key difference between the Jaffa and Bloom/Pangle factions is over Strauss's view of human wisdom. Jaffa emphasizes that the philosophers as philosophers never dispelled the mystery of Being, leaving space for the possibility of revelation's truth. Bloom and Pangle seem to claim to possess an amoral wisdom associated with atheism.

The Thomists
Many Christians and Jews have also benefited from Strauss's writing. He is indirectly and partly responsible for a revival of Thomistic/natural law thinking among some American conservatives. Some, such as Michael Novak, argue that Thomas Aquinas was "the first Whig," and that the American founding and economic freedom can be located and defended within a Thomistic framework. Novak's Catholicism does cause him to give capitalism one cheer, not two. But one cheer, he adds, is all it needs for justification as a merely economic system.

Other American Catholic thinkers are more suspicious of America's foundation, and they use their synthesis of reason and revelation to deepen the nation's first principles. Perhaps chief among these is the convert Richard John Neuhaus, who proclaimed that now is "the Catholic moment" in American political thought even before he became a Catholic. Part of the argument among Catholic conservatives concerns the meaning of the best political book written by a Catholic American adherent of natural law, John Courtney Murray's *We Hold These Truths* (1960). Some say Murray was rather uncritically American, and a few American Catholic traditionalists criticize him for his "Americanism." Others notice that Murray self-consciously modeled his project on Lincoln's. He aimed to transform American principles through a friendly reinterpretation from the perspective of the Catholic tradition, one much older, deeper, and more rational than America's own. Only through the integration of their principles into the creationist metaphysics of Thomistic natural law can Americans give a rational, plausible account of their conviction that all human beings are free persons under God.

What Is Conservatism?

American conservatism has tended to define itself in opposition to liberalism. But the forms of conservative thought I have considered, with exception of extreme libertarianism, do share some positive qualities. These include the location of the source of human progress not in technological change, environmental alteration, or political transformation but in the individual soul, and so in the development of character for the practice of virtue, the exercise of personal responsibility. It is not the scientists, technicians, or even philosophers but priests, prophets, poets, and lawgivers who most truly benefit human beings, and the order they establish under God, indispensable as it is for worthy and happy human lives, is worth fighting to conserve.

11

Tocqueville on Administration and for Administrators

Alexis de Tocqueville's *Democracy in America*, written in the 1830s, remains the best book on the American way of life. Tocqueville describes that way of life as democratic or egalitarian, but not completely so. He shows that the Americans love not only equality, but liberty, and he writes to defend that love of liberty against egalitarian or democratic excesses. His view is that the development of what we call public administration might well be one of those excesses. The spirit that guides the science of administration, devoted as it is to the efficiency or control that comes with the imposition of impersonal or egalitarian rules to regulate all of human life, is naturally opposed by the spirited love of liberty.

I have two purposes. The first is to consider what Tocqueville says about administration. *Democracy* has two volumes, and his approach to administration changes somewhat from volume 1 to volume 2, because he changes his view somewhat about the chief threat to liberty from democracy. I go on to consider what is most important about what Tocqueville says for American public administrators, his explanation of why Americans continue to find liberty lovable. That knowledge is indispensable for using one's political discretion well, for doing what one can to perpetuate human liberty in our time.

Administrative Decentralization versus
Tyranny of the Majority
In volume one, the main threat to liberty is called "tyranny of the majority." An activist majority might suppress minority dissent and individual resistance. Tocqueville's concern here is primarily that of the American Framers as expressed in *The Federalist*. With the danger of majority faction in mind, he describes and praises the Americans' "administrative decentralization." What he really praises is their administrative ineptitude, their lack of a science of administration. He says that "in the United States the majority, though it often has a despot's tastes and instincts, still lacks the most improved instruments of tyranny" (262).[1]

Tocqueville holds that tyranny of the majority is the American theory of government. There is and ought to be "no power capable of resisting" the majority's will as expressed in the legislature. Not "even the authority of reason" can resist, because the majority "claims to be the unique organ of reason" (89). The distinction between rational and majority rule is undemocratic. So the majority is limited only by the limits it imposes on its own will, by action it decides not to, cannot, or cannot imagine itself taking.

The Americans so far have neither the inclination nor the ability to regulate all of life according to the majority's sovereign will. The majority is "ignorant of how art might increase its scope" of power, of how an efficient, centralized administration might allow it more fully to exercise control (263). The majority suffers, from a purely democratic perspective, from a failure of thought and imagination.

In America, the "sovereign commands" of the majoritarian "central government" are "carried out by agents who often do not depend upon it and cannot be given direction every minute." They are the relatively independent and incompetent officials of local administration. They function as "so many hidden reefs retarding or dividing the flood of the popular will" (262–63). As long as the Americans leave administration decentralized with independent local officials, they will not be able to regulate effectively the details of individual lives. Endeavors requiring "continual care and rigorous exactitude for success" are usually beyond the competence and focus of American administrators (92). So America suffers from tyranny of the majority much more in principle than in practice.

Tocqueville finds wisdom, even if unconscious, in the American majority's lack of concern with details. In fact, no "central power . . . can . . . alone see to all the details of the life of a great nation" (91). That "task exceeds human strength." But Tocqueville also says it is possible to impose "an external uniformity" on people's behavior. Such success leads one to love uniformity "for itself without reference to its objectives" (91). Administrative efficiency becomes valued for its own sake, and all disorder is feared indiscriminately. Here we cannot help but think of the dissidents', Václav Havel's and Aleksandr Solzhenitsyn's, description of communist tyranny, which aimed simply to eradicate diversity or plurality from the world. The particularly democratic temptation, an extreme version of which we saw in communist ideology, is to combine the administrator's scientific propensity to increase the scope of his comprehension and control by submitting everything to impersonal rules with the egalitarian view that justice means treating everyone in the same way. The dissidents report that Communism achieved external conformity, but hardly ever genuine belief in the lie of ideology.[2]

Administrative centralization really can impose order on the details of daily life. It can "maintain the status quo." It can, in effect, put people to sleep, a condition "which administrators are in the habit of calling good order and public tranquility." But such administrative imposition "excels at preventing, not at doing." When personal responsibility and resolute action are required, government is "reduced to impotence" (91). Administrative stability is actually unstable, because it undermines the capacity of a particular people and particular individuals to respond effectively to the changes which will inevitably challenge them. Men will not act responsibly unless they are regarded as free. They are animated by self-direction far more than by obedience to rules not of their own making (92). A nation that has abandoned disorderly freedom for administratively-imposed uniformity is "ready for conquest." It lacks the "public virtues" that inspire personal resistance, because its inhabitants are already "subjects," not "citizens" (94).

So Tocqueville has both a negative and positive teaching on administrative decentralization, which he prefers for its "*political* advantages," not its administrative ones (93). Negatively, he praises its inefficiency for limiting the will of the majority, for preventing tyranny. Positively, he sees that that same inefficient inattention to detail arouses "civic spirit," giving citizens enough freedom to take pride in and responsibility for their own affairs. He observes the paradox that "In America, the force behind the state is much less well regulated, less enlightened, and less wise, but it is a hundred times more powerful than in Europe." The source of that power is personal effort: "Without doubt there is no other country on earth where people make such great efforts to achieve social prosperity." Individuals associate voluntarily to take responsibility for what administrators do not: "I know of no other people who have founded so many schools or such efficient ones, or churches more in touch with the religious needs of the inhabitants, or municipal roads better maintained" (92). Institutions suit people's needs because they are popularly originated and maintained.

Because in America the government's "means of action" or administration "are limited," individuals know they can and must rely largely on themselves. The "efforts of private individuals combine with those of the authorities" to "accomplish things which the most concentrated and vigorous administration would be unable to achieve" (95). Administrative decentralization blurs the line between and so combines public and private action. Tocqueville gives the example of the posse, or "inhabitants of a county . . . spontaneously forming committees with the object of catching the criminal and handing him over to the courts." Because local authorities have so few means for securing criminal justice, people know they cannot be "mere spectators" if justice is to be done (96).

In Europe, Tocqueville says, government's aim is to administer justice impersonally through the use of centralized authority. Local citizens need do and can do nothing. So they take no interest in or responsibility for the punishment of criminals, and a "public official stands for force," not "for right" (95). In America, by contrast, the police, prosecutors, and so forth are few in number, limited in power, and inefficient in method. "Nonetheless," Tocqueville observes, "I doubt whether in any country crime so seldom escapes punishment." Because local citizens share in the administration of justice, the criminal "becomes an enemy of the human race and every human being is against him" (96). The law stands for right, not mere force. The paradox is that when justice is connected with personal responsibility, it then seems less personal, or less merely the arbitrary will of those with power.

The source of this particularly American efficiency is not "uniformity or permanence of outlook, minute care of details, or perfection of administrative procedures." It lies in the "robust," because "somewhat wild" or disorderly, "striving and animation" of free citizens (92–93). Tocqueville contrasts the French "commune" with the American "township." In the former, thanks to Napoleonic centralization, the "accounting system is excellent," but people are "overtaken by such invincible apathy that society there seems to vegetate rather than live." They have no reason to give any thought to and so are mired in "profound ignorance of their true interests." The American townships have "untidy budgets lacking all uniformity," but also "an enlightened, active, and enterprising population." Tocqueville is astonished by the connection between the Americans' disorderly finances and their prosperity, and between the "immaculate budget" of the French and their "wretchedness" (92–93n.51).

Tocqueville remembers that the purpose of "good government is to ensure the welfare of a people and not to establish a certain order in the midst of their misery." So he "gladly" accepts the disorder and neglect of administrative decentralization, "compensated" as it is "by so many benefits" (93n.51). This robust resistance to order can be understood really to be resistance to tyranny of the majority. Individuals are confident enough of their own judgments to be patriotic without submitting blindly, to unite around "common interest," including tyranny's resistance, and to be willfully aroused against uniformity or homogenizing egalitarianism as an end in itself (96). But this spirit of resistance strengthens, not weakens, the individual's attachment to government. The combination of his own responsible efforts with those of administrators means that he can take pride in, or not feel detached from, what is achieved in the name of the public good (93).

But Tocqueville means to leave us fearful about the future of human liberty in America. Liberty seems to depend on a combination of administrative ineptitude and some deficiency in egalitarian imagination. There is every reason to anticipate what actually happened in American history. The science of administration would improve, increasingly more of the details of life would be subject to centralized administration in the name of efficiency and egalitarian justice, and the imagination would conceive of more possibilities for government regulation. Tocqueville says that the combination of administrative centralization and America's democratic political institutions could well produce a "despotism...more intolerable than in any of the absolute monarchies of Europe. One would have to go over into Asia to find anything with which to compare it" (263). The efficient, detailed implementation of majority will, so praised by the Progressives of our century and found at the core of our distinction between political will and administrative science, Tocqueville compares to Oriental despotism.

As Tocqueville explains, "no nations are more liable to fall under the yoke of administrative centralization than those with a democratic social condition" (96). There is an obvious, overwhelming connection between democracy and centralization. Democratization reduces the complexity of aristocratic social order to "nothing . . . but equal individuals mingled in a common mass" (97). After the abolition of social distinctions or diversity in the name of equality, there seems to be no foundation for resistance to the centralization of all power in the government that represents all equally. The spirit of democracy opposes the spirit of decentralization, because the latter depends upon and perpetuates a spirited resistance to uniformity, upon what Tocqueville regards as the aristocratic love of human particularity, the love of some particular human beings to the exclusion of them all.

The Americans and the English, Tocqueville observes, have a prejudice in favor of "local freedom" because they did not have the leveling, centralizing revolution of the French. The French Revolution was consistently motivated by hatred of everything aristocratic, and the Americans do not see that their local institutions are really, in part, aristocratic inheritances. They inconsistently incorporate them into their democratic chauvinism (97–98). Tocqueville makes it extremely hard to see why administrative decentralization will not decay over time in favor of a more consistently egalitarian or uniform conception of justice.

Tocqueville's Ambivalence

We also leave Tocqueville's laudatory account of administrative decentralization in volume one somewhat confused. The danger it countered is said to be an overbearing majority, which is limited only by administrative ineptitude. But Tocqueville also worries about the danger of an enervated, apathetic citizenry, about its inability to resist the tyranny of a meddlesome central government acting in the majority's name. Is the primary danger popular activism against minorities and individuals? Or is it popular apathy or spiritlessness? Is the tyranny to be feared an aroused majoritarianism? Or is it a seemingly impersonal central authority imposing uniform rules on a docile, willless, increasingly massified population?

The question of which form of tyranny or despotism is the greater danger must be answered in order to evaluate administrative decentralization. If it is tyranny of the majority, the result, finally, is ambivalence, and one might question the extent of Tocqueville's praise of local activism. *The Federalist*, for example, seems to be more on the side of administrative centralization than not, despite its inclination to leave many details to state and local government. Tyranny of the majority, for its authors, is more likely on the state and local level, where homogeneous majorities readily find themselves and where there are no barriers to their oppression.

Against that tyranny, its racism, sexism, meddlesome religious moralism, and so forth, much administrative control has moved to Washington over the years, arguably to some extent in accord with the intent of the Framers.

The greater professional training or expertise of national administrators also arguably produces more of a devotion to justice and rights than the wild, "redneck" chauvinism that sometimes animates local administrators. Although local populations in America may be relatively enlightened, are they really as enlightened as professional administrators? Tocqueville praises the posse, but we also know about lynchings. He does mention the "gross instances of social indifference and neglect" sometimes encountered in America, and even rare "major blemishes" that "appear completely at variance with the surrounding civilization" (92).

But such inconveniences, although hardly minor and certainly unjust, are worth bearing if the main threat to freedom is apathy. Local activism, even with its incompetence and limited but genuine majoritarian tyranny, must be maintained against the democratic grain of centralization. Tocqueville's suggestion, in this light, is that *The Federalist* was simply wrong about what is most required to perpetuate human liberty in America.

Apathetic, Despotic Degradation

Volume 2 of *Democracy* resolves the tension between the twin dangers of activism and apathy. There Tocqueville is not at all concerned with aroused majoritarianism, and he no longer refers to the tyranny of the majority. He is now concerned only with the unprecedented despotism that may come when individuals surrender control of the details of their lives, and so responsibility for and even thought about their futures, to gentle, apparently benevolent schoolmaster-administrators (691–93). That "*general apathy*" is "the fruit of individualism" (735n.AA), the malady of the heart, characteristic of democracy, that causes one to be incapable of love or hate (506–08). Tocqueville says "our efforts" should be directed not primarily against despotism but against the apathy that engenders it (735n.AA).

Individualism, Tocqueville says, is fundamentally the result of a "misguided judgment": The social, heart-enlarging experiences of human beings make them more miserably discontented than anything else (506–07). Human beings would be better off without those experiences. So individualism is a judgment in favor of the brutish contentment that comes with total unconcern for the future in Rousseau's state of nature. Tocqueville sees that democratic thought culminates logically in Rousseau's theoretical negation of all human distinctiveness, and his suggestion is that democratic practice moves in the direction of that thought, unless resisted by the artful efforts of lovers of human liberty.

Tocqueville's change in outlook from volume one to volume two seems to mirror American history, or the progress of democracy. The Framers thought the main danger to rights or liberty would be an overbearing majority. But we today are not particularly concerned about the specter of class warfare, demagogues rousing people into a frenzy, or even fundamentalist tyranny. The few card-carrying members of the ACLU who are still mainly animated by such concerns seem quaintly out of touch. Most analysts today "fear an apathetic or disabled majority that does not claim its rights or cannot exercise them."[3] Those on the Right worry about dependency, drugs, welfare, and the middle-class, and so about individuals who cannot or will not take responsibility for their own lives. Those on the Left complain about individuals so withdrawn and insensitive that they are incapable of acting on behalf on the unfortunate.

Almost everyone seems distressed about the low turnout of voters, the lack of citizen involvement, and the stupefying power of television and popular music to absorb people in "private fantasies" or what Rousseau called reveries. Those on both the Left and Right, although obviously not everyone, also criticize the growing influence of the New Age, therapeutic culture, which aims to keep individuals from being touched by their experiences of their individuality by showing them, Buddhist-fashion, that such anxious and contingent experiences of particularity are an illusion. Individualism, we see, is much more of a problem in our time than in Tocqueville's, and we marvel at his prescience about democracy's development.

Human action, Tocqueville observes, is becoming more regular, uniform, and methodical. "Variety is disappearing from the human race" (615). Not only are human beings behaving more similarly and predictably, even the difference between human and nonhuman reality may be in the process of disappearing. Democratic theorists prefer deterministic or systematic explanations of human behavior, ones that deny or abstract from human liberty and responsibility. The main reason for their preference is that such explanations are homogeneous or completely egalitarian. Not only do they not privilege the thought and action of particular, extraordinary individuals, they claim to show that what animates human beings is no different from what animates all the animals or all that exists (493–96). Such explanations, Tocqueville says, perniciously and untruly deny or miss genuine manifestations of human liberty (451–52, 495, 544). But he also acknowledges that systematic or deterministic science is becoming more true as democracy develops (494). Human beings are progressively less likely to demand to be recognized or to be recognizable as individuals (626, 631–32).

In aristocracies, human beings were distinguished in many ways, and the aristocrat's sense of his individuality or liberty was strong and amply supported, although it was not unlimited. So the aristocrat, Tocqueville says, conceived of the idea of rights, a proud assertion of independence against others and the social whole (663). That idea is what "is rapidly disappearing from men's minds." Replacing it in Tocqueville's time is "the idea of the omnipotence and sole authority of society at large" (669). The personal idea, one that defends one's particular liberty and responsibility, is being replaced by the impersonal one, the one compatible with and served well by administrative science or bureaucracy. The idea of rights, originating in the aristocrat's proud experience of ruling himself and others, is replaced by one which suggests that no one in particular is responsible or rules.

Aristocrats, Tocqueville says, do justice or more than justice to natural human distinctions. But they are so enamored with human particularity or inegalitarian individuality that they find it almost impossible to conceive of general ideas, ways of thinking that reveal what all human beings have in common with each other and with all that exists (439). So the "notion of a uniform rule imposed equally on all members of the body social seems to have been strange to men's thoughts in ages of aristocracy" (668). It did not occur to them that it might be more just and efficient to impose uniform rules on everyone, and so their science of administration or bureaucracy could not progress.

With the decay of aristocratic social distinctions in the face of egalitarian skepticism, the dissolution of "the ancient fabric of European society," human beings have become both less different and less aware of differences. They have come to think readily, too readily, with general ideas (437). So European governments "nowadays . . . wear themselves out imposing uniform customs and laws on populations with nothing yet in common" (689). Their thought is oriented by an imagined uniformity not yet in existence. Their general or impersonal ideas do not yet adequately describe human reality. Their ideas are in part impositions which aim to eradicate the diversity which they cannot comprehend.

Aristocrats intensely love and hate particular human beings. They are strongly attached to some to the unjust or arbitrary exclusion of others. They often cannot even recognize the humanity of nonaristocrats, those outside their circle of concern (563–64). The particularly democratic love is not of particular human beings, but of the general idea or abstract principle "equality." Only God can love all human beings equally and intensely; only He can see us all as we really are. For human beings, limited as we are in thought, feeling, and imagination, love becomes less particular or intense as its scope increases (437). Corresponding to the democratic love of equality is "hatred of privilege" (672). Democrats hate love which prefers or privileges one or some over others. They hate human love as it actually exists, which is why they judge in favor of individualism, an apathetic, passionless existence. That democratic hatred, Tocqueville observes, actually grows with progress toward equality, because "amid the general uniformity, the slightest dissimilarity seems shocking" (673). The democratic love is for the perfection of uniformity. So its hatred is for anything that cannot be comprehended and controlled by impersonal, administrative rules. The hatred of privilege favors the concentration or centralization of power in government. Whatever is conceded to "the state" is taken from unequal individuals. Because the state or the sovereign impersonally represents us all equally, its power does not arouse hatred or envy (673). The more it controls, the more uniform our lives will become.

The great danger to liberty in democratic times is that the devotion of democrats and that of the "central government" are the same. The government "worships uniformity" because it is infinitely easier to subject "all men indiscriminately to the same rule" than to make rules that actually "suit men" in their diversity. Both the government and democratic citizens hate unequal, disorderly manifestations of human liberty. So they have "a secret and permanent bond of sympathy," forming a "community of feeling" against "individual independence" (673). They both feel that the experience of liberty is not a human good. The increase of centralized, homogenized, governmental control over all the details of human life is the "natural" progress of democracy (674). The "instinct for centralization" has been "the one permanent feature" of democratic development. So "one can say that the older a democratic society, the more centralized will its government be" (672n.1).

Tocqueville adds that "the art of despotism" in democratic times has been "simplified," even "reduced to a single principle" (679). Government's justification for the centralization of power is the love of equality. Rulers either must actually have that love or convince citizens that they do. The pursuit of equality is the fraud used by despots in democratic times to maximize their own power. It allows them to control their subjects more completely than subjects had ever been controlled before. The government's professed devotion to egalitarian uniformity leads "those same men who from time to time have upset a throne and trampled kings beneath their feet to bend without resistance to the slightest wishes of some clerk" (688).

The Science of Administration
The method used to pursue the egalitarian and despotic goal of complete uniformity is "the science of administration." Tocqueville notes the "immense improvements" in that science by the European governments of his time. He "assert[s] that there is no country in Europe in which public administration has become not only more centralized but also more impulsive and minute." It "meddles" in affairs formerly regarded as private; it extends indefinitely the sphere of its control. With the science of administration "the state itself . . . increasingly takes control of the humblest citizen and directs his behavior even in trivial matters" (680). Charity, education, and religion have been brought under administrative control. "[F]unctionaries" have taken responsibility "for forming the feelings and shaping the ideas of each generation" (681). Through them "princes" now do more than govern: "They seem to hold themselves responsible for the behavior and fate of subjects as individuals." Through guidance and instruction, princes "will, if necessary, make them happy against their will" (681). The aim of the prince and his administrative functionaries is to produce perfectly orderly, predictable subjects, to eradicate the willfulness that comes with discontent. The discipline imposed here is that of the "schoolmaster," the expert who tells his students what to think and feel for their own good (681, 691).

The despotic use of the science of administration "degrades rather than torments" subjects by depriving them of their free or willful exercise of personal responsibility. By "cover[ing] the whole of social life with a network of petty, complicated rules that are both minute and uniform," it "daily makes the exercise of free choice less useful and rarer . . . , rob[bing] each citizen of the proper use of his own facilities" (692). Such a people "slowly falls below the level of humanity," because human beings are defined by their exercise of their liberty, by their spirited, responsible and sometimes immoderate choices (694). Tocqueville says that the goal of "[t]his brand of orderly, gentle, peaceful slavery" is to "entirely relieve" people "from the trouble of thinking and all the cares of living" (692).

That people might gradually surrender their thought about and responsibility for their futures to schoolmaster-administrators for their own good suggests that the psychological explanation of love of equality given so far has been too abstract. Not only do democratic citizens hate the manifestations of the unequal individuality of others, they come to experience their own individuality as hateful. The democratic destruction of aristocratic hierarchy and other social ties leaves the individual "both independent and weak." That new independence fills the individual temporarily with "confidence and pride," but soon he feels his weakness and vulnerability, his need for help from others to secure his existence. But with the dissolution of social ties and duties, and so the deterioration of love, his "fellows" seem equally "impotent and cold" (672).

The impotent individual turns to that "huge entity," centralized government, that "alone stands out above the universal level of abasement" (672). He expects government to do what his friends, fellow citizens, and family used to do. But finally he is looking for more than day care, social security, and welfare. The individual in democratic ages becomes obsessed with time, because he has been skeptically deprived of various aristocratic illusions about immortality. Everything seems mutable; despite his constant calculation the future is beyond his control, and he cannot divert himself effectively from the inevitability of death (537). He is "frightened by" his apparently "limitless independence." His unsupported individuality wears him out and eventually becomes hateful (444).

Because thoughts about the future seem to do nothing but make them miserable, democratic individuals "easily fall back into a complete and brutish indifference about the future" (548). They readily conclude that they are better off surrendering all calculation about the future to administrators. Finally, they would rather not be touched by awareness of their mortality, their individuality; they would rather lose themselves in the moment. As Rousseau says, the most egalitarian conclusion is that human beings are better off when they are brutishly unaware of time.

The best Tocquevillian analyst of American democracy in our time has been the philosopher-physician-novelist Walker Percy. According to Percy, Tocqueville's core observation was that the Americans are Cartesians without ever having read a word of Descartes. Their view of the world is pop Cartesian.[4] They understand the world and themselves in terms of a popularized, deterministic science articulated by experts. These experts, counselors, therapists, administrators, Phil Donahue, Carl Sagan, and so forth, say that human beings are no different from the other animals. They should be happy in good or prosperous environments, and miserable in bad or impoverished ones. Any experience that causes them to be miserable in the midst of prosperity should be dismissed as a misery-producing illusion. Therapy means changing the environment that produces such unproductive moods.[5]

Tocqueville himself suggests how democracy produces the rule of scientific experts. He says that democracy makes the individual too intellectually weak, too uncertain and disoriented, to resist public opinion. The rule of public opinion seems not to be undemocratic, because it appears to be the rule of no one in particular (434–36). But democratic public opinion itself is shaped by its tendency to be expressed in the language of impersonal or deterministic science (477–82). That language is articulated by experts, who claim not to rule on the basis of their own judgments but only to express the objective authority of science. The expert shaping of public opinion also appears to be the rule of no one in particular.

Percy makes clear what individuals attempt to surrender when they give up their personal sovereignty or responsibility to impersonal expertise. He says what terrifies people most is not sex or crime or poverty. They have trouble "knowing who they are or what to do with themselves." Their perplexity increases when they are not doing what "*They*, the experts" say they should be doing. The experts cannot explain why wealthy, intelligent, and attractive people should be miserable and unproductive for "no apparent reason."[6] The pop Cartesian experts are the *they* the philosopher

Martin Heidegger describes: *"The 'they' do not permit us anxiety in the face of death."*[7] Their expertise means to keep one from being touched by one's awareness of mortality. Their judgment is that that experience is not good for human beings.

According to Percy, the Cartesian experts mean to deprive the individual of what constitutes his freedom, his sovereignty, his capacity to live in the light of the truth. Percy's own judgment is Tocqueville's: Such personal experiences lie at the core of human liberty, and human beings really can live well with some help while facing death. Percy notices that the experts have not been able to deprive Americans of the anxious restlessness of self-conscious mortality, and Tocqueville himself describes the Americans as anxious and restless, even melancholic and disgusted with life, in the midst of prosperity (535–38). Tocqueville and Percy describe the failure, so far, of the expert science of administration completely to shape human experience and take control of the details of particular lives. What Phil Donahue, Carl Sagan, the politically-correct administrator and so forth say does not yet conform to what Americans actually experience.

Percy denies that experts can eradicate human misery. They end up making some Americans, at least, feel more miserably dislocated than ever before by depriving them of language through which they can articulate their personal experiences of self or soul. Tocqueville similarly writes of the tendency of democracy to eradicate the theological and metaphysical dimensions of language (477), and of the Americans' deepening inability to divert themselves from the needs of the soul (535–38). His fear, in fact, is that the Americans may well surrender the details of their lives, their responsibility for the future, to administrators precisely because their lives have become so anxious and restless (548). Because the Americans find the experiences of individuality, of self-conscious mortality, to be so hard, they may willingly give them up in favor of a life that is too easy truly to be human. Because they sometimes find liberty hateful, they may come to prefer complete equality, which is necessarily subhuman.

Tocqueville imagines the perfection of unprecedented, democratic despotism, the despot's control of all the details of peaceful, orderly, subhuman lives. Allied with and at the service of the despot is the administrative scientist or expert, who holds that such control is for the individual's benefit. The individual, the expert asserts, would be better off living with a childish, irresponsible indifference for the future. He would be better off freed from the miserable burden of anxious calculation, and from being touched by his knowledge of his mortality. He should live only in the enjoyment of the moment, and he should be freed from those restless experiences which deprive him of that enjoyment (692).

Opposed to the despot and the expert is the lover of liberty for its own sake, in spite of that misery. In that category Tocqueville places only a few, "the true friends of liberty and of human dignity," who artfully resist the movement toward democracy (699, 674). He does not favor an unjust and futile attempt to reinvigorate aristocracy, but only the perpetuation of the liberty that is possible in democratic ages (695). He says "The individual should be allowed to keep the little freedom, strength, and originality left to him. His position in the face of society should be raised and supported. Such, I think, should be the chief aim of any legislator in the age opening before us" (701). The task of the legislator or statesman is to provide individuality with assistance or support, because if left unsupported it becomes unendurable.

The Love of Liberty

The public administrator, on the basis of his scientific or technical education and his professional pride, tends to become a pop Cartesian expert.[8] But if he reads Tocqueville, he might become a true friend of liberty or a statesman. Insofar as he is able to exercise independent judgment or discretion, he will act either to use his expertise to relieve citizens of their freedom and responsibility, or he will do what he can to support and encourage experiences of individuality or personal responsibility. What can be done to keep liberty lovable for Americans? That is the question the American engaged in political life, including the administrator, ought always to ask. Knowledge of what makes liberty lovable for human beings, along with the actual love of liberty, are necessary supplements to the science of administration in the education of public administrators in a nation dedicated to liberty.

Tocqueville observes that the Americans do love liberty, because they are able to exercise it in the context of the fortunate perpetuation of institutions inherited from aristocratic ages. The first Americans were English, and they brought with them England's "free institutions and virile mores," which originated in aristocratic pride. These institutions, fortunately, were not leveled by any "great democratic revolution" or "war between the various classes" (675). The Americans are in the crucial respect considerably less democratic than the French. "The American destiny," Tocqueville asserts, "is unusual; they have taken from the English aristocracy the idea of individual rights and a taste for local freedom, and they have been able to keep both these things because they have had no aristocracy to fight" (676). What Tocqueville says about the extreme consequences of democracy's development does not yet apply to the Americans. Meddlesome, puerile administration has perfected itself in Europe, not America.

Tocqueville discusses the Americans' inheritance of the "free institutions" of local government as part of their "combat" against individualism. He does so in part 2 of volume 2 of *Democracy*, where his subject is the effect of the movement toward democracy on love or the heart, and so also the maladies specific to democracy which threatens the heart's functioning. It is because love of equality opposes human love as it actually exists that democratic progress, unresisted, culminates in individualism. The Americans engage in such resistance or combat because they are not simply democrats. They love not only equality but liberty, each other, and God.[9]

The Americans actually employ two weapons in their combat against individualism. The first is "free institutions," the second is "interest rightly understood." Free, local institutions are the practical, political combat employed by "the lawgivers of America," largely the English (509–13). Interest rightly understood, the doctrine of American moralists, is theoretical (525–28). The latter presupposes the success of the former. Moralistic theory supports American political practice, aiming to help secure the legislators' work.

Both forms of combat aim to enlarge the American heart. How free institutions do this is not hard to see. But the doctrine of interest is explicitly and pridefully heartless. We have to consider how a pridefully heartless doctrine aids the enlargement of the heart. The moralist's doctrine, it turns out, is less concerned with interest itself than with the relationships among interest, pride, and love in a comprehensive strategy to resist democracy's antiliberal excesses. We have to consider the first form of combat to find the place of the second.

Tocqueville begins his chapter on free institutions by showing the connection between individualism and despotism. Here he anticipates *Democracy*'s conclusion. The "vices" of despotism, which the despot calls virtues, contract the heart or keep human beings from loving one another. All the despot needs to maintain his power unimpeded is apathy or "indifference" (509).

Democratic people "have a particular need" for the experience of political freedom to resist despotism's progress. They must be compelled, against their inclination, "to take part in public affairs," to be citizens. When "common affairs are treated in common," the individual learns the limits of his self-sufficiency. He "notices he is not as independent of his fellows as he used to suppose." He needs them, and to get their help he must help them. Political indifference is not in one's interest or even possible (510).

What begins as calculation of interest ends in love. The individual calculates that he gains the cooperation of others most effectively with "their goodwill and affection." He sees that it is in his interest to be loved by others. But that love will not come unless he acts to "disguise" his pride, contempt, and egoism, the pretentious passions that constitute his perception of self-sufficiency. By fooling others, he cannot help but fool himself to some extent. "Those frigid passions," Tocqueville says, "that keep hearts asunder must then retreat and hide at the back of consciousness." The individual compelled to act as if he were a citizen actually becomes one (510).

The free institutions of local government, of which decentralized administration might be considered a part, artfully create ties that exist much more readily or seemingly naturally in an aristocracy. One's imagination and so one's heart is extended to and filled by others. This awakening of the social passions, love and pride, affects human beings unequally. More pride is aroused in some than in others, and the extraordinary pride of a few arouses love in many. This aristocratic orientation becomes obvious when Tocqueville notices that "[u]nder free government most public officials are elected" (510).

The possibility of winning elections attracts "men whose great gifts and aspirations are too closely circumscribed in private life," those with the ability and prideful passion to distinguish themselves. This ambition also "makes a man care for his fellows"; he needs their votes. Again calculation turns readily into affection and love. Tocqueville even says that the candidate "often finds his self-interest in forgetting about himself." Self-interest and selflessness are intertwined, because the best way to appear to care is actually to care (510).

The stimulation by election of political ambition is a social and so heart-enlarging passion. The "[e]agerness to be elected" is what most powerfully "forges permanent links among a great number of citizens who otherwise might have remained forever strangers to one another." The natural aristocrats, those with a prideful love of human liberty, create the ties that combat individualism. Those who are less inclined to be content with the individualist's apolitical life attract the political interest and affection of those who are more content. Aristocratic or political interest and pride arouse democratic love (510).

The Americans have incorporated their aristocratic inheritance of the institutions of local government into their view of democracy. It is what gives them a relatively liberal view of democracy. But like their chauvinistic attachment to administrative decentralization, it remains vulnerable to egalitarian criticism. America over time has centralized in the name of justice. Largely gone are the particularistic and passionate local institutions Tocqueville described. Local democracy is activist democracy. It readily arouses pride and love and so difference, inequality, hatred, and injustice. National democracy—because it is more consistently impersonal and egalitarian or just—tends to be apathetic democracy.

Local democracy depends more on personal responsibility, the exercise of which is somewhat unpredictable. National democracy depends more on the predictable uniformity of bureaucracy. Politically-inspired love and pride have almost disappeared, because Americans can no longer connect their interests to effective political action. They too rarely have the political experiences that readily turn calculation into affection.

Arguably, administrators today should use their discretion to promote plans to "devolve" some of the responsibility of government to the states and localities. The implementation of such plans may well produce some injustice. As Tocquevillians, perhaps we can say that they are the price one pays to arouse some political passion, and to restore political liberty. But Tocqueville was especially worried about American racism, which he viewed as a monstrous form of injustice, and he saw the connection between it and the states' decentralizing assertion of self-government. He would have welcomed almost any effective remedy to it (355–63).

Perhaps Tocqueville might have recommended the statesmanship of Speaker Newt Gingrich. Gingrich, in his first speech as speaker, praised the centralization or nationalization of the 1960s that aimed at racial justice. He made it clear that today's decentralization presupposes the success of that centralization. Returning power to the states and localities today will be much less likely to produce particularly racist policy.

But Tocqueville might also have been very skeptical of any attempt to return vitality to local institutions once it has been lost. His effort was largely to preserve the aristocratic inheritances in America that had survived the transition to democracy. He did not recommend the creation of new, free institutions. Because of their habitual skepticism in the service of equality, democrats lack the imaginary resources for such creativity (445, 485). So far only a few observers have noticed that Gingrich's American revolution or realignment, if it eventually succeeds, would be the first directed against equality's excesses.

How the doctrine of interest well understood contributes to the Americans' proud love of liberty is more difficult to see. This doctrine, which Tocqueville describes as the teaching of American moralists, is that everything human beings do should be the product of enlightened calculation in pursuit of material enjoyment. The Americans enjoy explaining that it accounts for all their activity: "It gives them pleasure to point out how an enlightened self-love continually leads them to help one another and disposes them freely to give part of their time and wealth for the good of the state" (526). They complacently think they show how citizenship need not depend on love or thoughtless self-sacrifice.

What the Americans enjoy explaining is that they are consistent thinkers and free actors. Their rational will is the basis of their independence. They have freed themselves from natural and imaginary propensities to be attached to others. They know the truth that every human being is separated from others by bodily need, and that life is nothing but doing what one can to satisfy one's own needs.

So Tocqueville makes it clear that the American doctrine is a form of boasting about one's liberty. Before their enlightenment, in aristocratic ages, human beings were unfree. Their imaginations formed illusory bonds of dependence. They were blinded by the illusions of love and duty, which aristocrats manipulated to control others. The result was injustice rooted in ignorance. The Americans use their minds, the democratic method of consistent, skeptical thinking, to dispel the illusions and liberate their wills to overcome injustice, each individual in his own case.

But Tocqueville contends that the Americans do not accurately explain why they do what they do. He says, with some irony, that they "often do themselves less than justice." He notices them sometimes abandoning themselves, "carried away" by natural impulses and really serving others. They are, like people "elsewhere," partly selfish and partly not (526). Interest may explain some, but never all, of what human beings do. From an aristocratic perspective, the Americans are inclined to be better or more selfless citizens than they say. The American's response to Tocqueville would be that Tocqueville does him less than justice. The American always resists the call of the heart. Despite the appearance of self-sacrifice, all his social and political relationships are his own construction and so within his own control.

We remember that Tocqueville had already explained how the heart-enlarging effects of the free institutions of local government transform the pursuit of interest. Given the effect of such experience, which makes their heartless moral doctrine inaccurate, why do American moralists support the doctrine at all? Why do they encourage the Americans, in effect, not to tell the whole truth about their experiences?

The American doctrine, as a form of boasting, is also a cover or disguise. Americans deny that they really love, but sometimes, as a result of their political involvement, they really do. The fact of their love offends their sense of liberty or pride. They do not want to acknowledge their dependence, what limits their liberty. So Tocqueville affirms the doctrine of interest because it allows the American to explain away the true effects of his heart-enlarging experiences. It verbally disguises his impulsive affection for others, aroused by his political life. By doing so, it makes it easier for him to have such experiences. His love need not seem to be incompatible with his pride. A heartless moral doctrine disguises and so protects what enlarges the heart.

Here again, public administrators might look to the example of Gingrich, to the prideful inadequacy of his public argument. He attempts to justify as many of his policy choices as possible according to the doctrine of interest, as good for the pursuit of prosperity and personal economic independence. But for him the doctrine is clearly a boast and a cover. His responsible, anti-bureaucratic choices exhibit a love of political liberty which no doctrine of enlightened self-interest could ever adequately articulate. Tocqueville shows why the speaker should be praised, not blamed, for not acknowledging his own and our dependence. Political theorists today sometimes see the connection between acknowledgments of dependence and apathy, but almost never do they see the one between prideful assertions of self-interest and active, and sometimes even selfless, citizenship.

But we cannot forget the interdependence of the two forms of combat against individualism. The doctrine of interest is praised by Tocqueville as a way of protecting local political life. In the absence of that life, the goodness of the prideful doctrine of interest becomes far more questionable. Tocqueville cannot help but notice the troubling inconsistency of the Americans' moralistic defense of their liberty. For them, liberty is the consistent pursuit of material enjoyment, but it is not enjoyment itself. Once one enjoys, one is no longer free, because one gives way to instinct or impulse, or gives up self-control. So the Americans seem to say proudly that they pursue enjoyment, but never enjoy. They seem to explain a nonmaterialistic motivation in materialistic terms. They say all there is bodily need, but their restless, insatiable pursuit of its satisfaction is evidence of their liberty from that need. But a life without enjoyment could hardly be lovable, and the attempt actually to live it makes the preference for apathetic individualism over liberty seem perfectly reasonable.

Religion and the Family

The doctrine of interest protects, in a largely democratic context, the heart-enlarging effects of America's lucky aristocratic inheritance of free, local political institutions. A wider glance at *Democracy's* volume 2 shows that the doctrine performs the same function for two other American inheritances, religion and the family. These institutions also fortunately enlarge the American heart and make liberty lovable. So they also combat individualism. They are also vulnerable to self-centered, democratic criticism of inegalitarian dependency generated by the imagination.

Tocqueville begins his description of the American application of the doctrine of interest rightly understood by saying that "However hard one may try to prove that virtue is useful, it will always be difficult to make a man live well if he will not face death" (528). He opposes the experts who would recommend the pursuit of enjoyment as a diversion from one's self-conscious mortality. He adds that the Americans actually agree with him.

Tocqueville observes, with irony, that Americans actually take pride in extending the doctrine of interest to their religious duties and their relationship with God. He notices that their view of religious practice is "so quiet, so methodical, and so calculated that it would seem that the head rather than the heart leads them to the altar." They calculate how best to achieve "eternal felicity," as if they could even bring that under their control. Their aim is to give the minimum amount of attention to religious duty and still gain eternal life. They do not want to sacrifice more than is necessary for the pursuit of happiness or enjoyment in this world (529–30).

The Americans' doctrine is, in effect, a proud denial that they either love God or are anxious about their contingency or mortality. Even God and death need not limit one's independence. They "affect no vulgar indifference to a future state," because they hold it is possible to plan for all of one's future (529). Obviously enough, if they really lived according to their doctrine they would not really be facing death.

Egalitarian skepticism dissolves even love of God. Christianity, as Tocqueville says, is a most egalitarian religion. All human beings are equal under God. But Christianity also teaches man's love of and dependence upon God, and his duties to others flow from that love. That attachment and dependence limit one's liberty, and they depend on evidence apparently generated by the imagination. They originate, in Tocqueville's own view, in the imaginative arousal of love made possible by aristocratic social conditions (439, 443–46, 483–84). So he strikingly calls the Americans' religion their "most precious inheritance from aristocratic times" (544). The best hope for the future of the love of God, which seems necessary if human beings are going to love one another and liberty itself, is to perpetuate whatever religion a particular democracy may have fortunately inherited.

Tocqueville affirms the Americans' application of the doctrine of interest to religion because it is not a true or complete description of their religious longing or action. The application is only largely true in the sense that interest may really be what usually leads human beings to religion. But interest never explains all of religious practice (529). The Americans' claim that they are free from anxiety about death and longing for God's love is a boast. That anxiety and longing are the main causes of their restlessness in the midst of prosperity. Their pursuit of enjoyment really is an increasingly less successful diversion from their increasingly anxious longing (535–38).

Tocqueville also observes the Americans acting as if they really do love God. On the seventh day they are able to rest, taking time to contemplate God and their souls. They are then temporarily but truly free from both calculation of interest and personal anxiety. They have some confidence, sometimes, that they are somehow immortal. That experience is a source of pride indispensable for the love of liberty or individuality (529, 542–45). The Americans' boast that they have reduced religion to the domain of interest actually protects their religious experiences from skeptically democratic criticism.

So public administrators today ought to see the truth in what has become the conservative argument that religious belief supports liberty and the pursuit of prosperity. The American claim to have reconciled the spirit of Christianity with that of capitalism is not altogether true. It is a boast and a cover, one to be protected. Administrators ought also to resist the welfare-state tendency to expand the reach of government in ways that constrain religious practice. Most of all, they ought not to let their love of egalitarian justice or impersonal efficiency undermine organized expressions of man's love of God.

Tocqueville also makes it clear enough that the family, even in its American, democratic form, is another aristocratic inheritance. His presentation of that fact is quite indirect. His initial emphasis is on how democracy has transformed relations among family members. In the short term, the movement toward democracy has increased familial love by liberating it from the proud reserve of aristocratic formalities (586–89).

But the development of democracy, as we see so clearly today, eventually threatens the family's very existence. It cannot be held together by love alone, and the love of one's particular family members is undermined by love of equality. The family is necessarily exclusive, and its existence will always be a barrier to the achievement of perfectly egalitarian justice.

Today the emphasis is often on the unjust subordination the family has imposed on women. Tocqueville's conclusion is that the superiority of

American women is the cause of the endurance of the American family (603). They submit, in his description, to a transformed but genuine form of patriarchy, justified by the doctrine of interest rightly understood. That doctrine causes the American view of marriage to be strangely unerotic. The Americans' distrust and disparagement of romantic love is another instance of their "continual sacrifice of pleasure for the sake of business," or their pursuit of prosperity for the sake of pleasure (592). The Americans explain that their pursuit is most efficient when labor is divided between men and women. "They have applied to the sexes the great principle of political economy which now dominates industry" (601).

Tocqueville observes that American women's work is in the home, the men's business and politics. But the husband still rules the family under the law, and the wife is socially subordinate and almost literally locked up in the home. The Americans do allow the women the choice of whom to marry, and even whether or not to marry. But they are educated to use their freedom well, and they know that marry they must if they are to secure what happiness and dignity is possible for them in this world. One reason American women are superior to American men is that they acknowledge freely that human beings must submit, or acknowledge their dependence, if they are to live well with their liberty (590–97).

American women, Tocqueville shows, humor the pride of men. But they know that male pride is really chauvinism, and they secretly view it with some contempt. Women are the source of morality and defenders of religion. They shape the souls of children and even their husbands. They assume the responsibility of socializing or humanizing men, making love and contentment possible in a vulgarly selfish age. So they are responsible for the perpetuation of human happiness and dignity by making life something more than liberty conceived as anxious restlessness ending only in death. By constraining liberty with love, they make liberty lovable (291, 592–93, 598, 600–03).

American men pay their women lip service, but in fact they are largely unaware of the extent of their dependence. They certainly do not acknowledge how anxious and miserable they would be without women's self-denying efforts. Their doctrine of interest rightly understood, with which they explain their family ties, is again a prideful cover, allowing them not to acknowledge the conjugal and familial love and sense of duty they really experience (594–603).

The family Tocqueville describes may be largely gone today, a victim of democracy's development, especially women's liberation. But it is not completely gone. Women still sacrifice more than men for the children's sake, and perhaps that is because they are more inclined by nature to do so. They still even humor male pride to some extent, and certainly men are still more reluctant to acknowledge their dependence. Even today's more egalitarian family is under attack, primarily in the name of the perfection of women's liberation. Government policy, driven mainly by equality and efficiency, is not the family's particular friend. Yet the natural superiority of women requires social and political support to be effective.

The sociologist David Popenoe has made the Tocquevillian observation that life has gotten both better and worse for Americans over the last generation. There has been genuine and rapid progress in the direction of justice defined as "inclusivity." One aspect of that progress has been the "legal, social, and financial emancipation of women." But there is also social and moral deterioration, more crime and greed, less trust, and a general confusion about moral standards. Families are failing, and more people are lonely. The average, middle class American is "more fearful, anxious, and unsettled," more full of "individual anguish," and so on balance less happy.[10]

There is now, as Tocqueville predicted, too unconstrained a perception of freedom or choice, too much of life is dissociated from the domain of social duty. Too much human experience, in effect, has been turned over to the doctrine of interest. This emotional detachment or movement toward individualism Popenoe traces primarily to the decline in the number of stable, affectionate nuclear families. If women are no longer defined primarily by the task of habituating or socializing children, it is unclear who in particular is charged with raising them. Most of all, today's parents cannot find adequate time to raise children.[11]

Public administrators should join the growing consensus that the strong, two-parent, heterosexual family is the best suited for preparing and sustaining individuals for the responsible exercise of liberty. The experiences of love and dependence are required for the proper development of the American mixture of personal independence and familial, political, and religious responsibility. "Recent sociological studies," William Galston summarizes, "confirm a strong correlation between family solidarity and the sense of obligation to a wider community or society." So the decline of the two-parent family produces "a growing subset of the population that cannot discharge the basic responsibilities of citizenship in a liberal democracy."[12]

Studies also show that, even for most adult Americans, family life remains the greatest source of happiness and personal satisfaction. A stable marriage, Popenoe notices, "is good for one's physical and mental health."[13] It limits one's restless anxiety with love. Men still need their wives to experience such order more than women need their husbands. Because familial love is still what makes life worth living for most Americans, administrators should do what they can to support it, even at the expense of equality and efficiency. They should do what they can to assist American women in employing their natural superiority in resisting democracy's inhuman or individualistic excesses.

Conclusion: Administration as Democratic Statesmanship

The Tocquevillian paradox is that excessive independence generates excessive dependence. So the modern, democratic process of liberation from all forms of authority in the name of equality seems to be culminating in bigger, more powerful, and more meddlesome government than ever before. What big government does, above all, is constrain individual choice, and it most readily grows when individuals feel especially in need of such constraint. Big government is welcomed by those who feel isolated, disoriented, and personally powerless, who lack the resources to choose well.[14]

Administrators cannot help but be inclined to administer, to control impersonally the lives of others in the name of justice and technical competence. But Tocqueville shows them why they should act against their administrative inclination on behalf of their love of human liberty. They should devote themselves to perpetuating personal responsibility in a quite impersonal and irresponsible time.

NOTES

1. The page numbers in parenthesis in the text refer to the Lawrence translation of *Democracy in America* (Alexis de Tocqueville, *Democracy in America*, ed. J. P. Mayer, trans. G. Lawrence [New York: Harper and Row, 1988]).

2. For an introduction to Solzhesityn's and Havel's dissident thought, see my "The Dissident Criticism of America," *The American Experiment: Essays on the Theory and Practice of Liberty*, ed. P. Lawler and R. Schaefer (Lanham, MD: Rowman and Littlefield, 1994).

3. Harvey C. Mansfield, Jr., *America's Constitutional Soul* (Baltimore: Johns Hopkins University Press, 1991), p. 177. This paragraph and the next are indebted to Mansfield's astute chapter 13.

4. Lewis Lawson and Victor A. Kramer, eds., *More Conversations with Walker Percy* (Jackson: University Press of Mississippi, 1991), pp. 232–33.

5. Most of Percy's analysis found here is taken from *Lost in the Cosmos: The Last Self-Help Book* (New York: Farrar, Straus, and Giroux, 1983). For elaboration, see my *"Lost in the Cosmos*: Walker Percy's Analysis of American Restlessness," *Poets, Princes and Private Citizens*, ed., J. Knippenberg and P. Lawler (Lanham, MD: Rowman and Littlefield, 1996).

6. Walker Percy, *The Thanatos Syndrome* (New York: Farrar, Straus, and Giroux, 1987), p. 88.

7. Martin Heidegger, *Being and Time*, trans. J. Macquarrie and E. Robinson (New York: Harper and Row, 1962), pp. 297–98.

8. See Michael W. Spicer, *The Founders, the Constitution, and Public Administration: A Conflict in World Views* (Washington: Georgetown University Press, 1995) with the refinements in Spicer's argument

suggested by Donald J. Maletz in his review (*The American Political Science Review 90* [March, 1996], pp. 205–06).

9. From this point onward, I draw upon my "Tocqueville on Pride, Interest, and Love," *Polity* 28 (Winter, 1995), pp. 217–36.

10. David Popenoe, "The Family Condition of America: Cultural Change and Public Policy," *Values and Public Policy*, ed. H. Aaron et al. (Washington, D.C.: The Brookings Institution, 1994), p. 90.

11. *Ibid.*, p. 104.

12. William A. Galston, "Liberal Virtues and the Formation of Civic Character," *Seedbeds of Virtue*, ed. M. Glendon and D. Blankenhorn (Lanham, MD: Madison Books, 1995), p. 56.

13. Popenoe, p. 98. See also James Q. Wilson, *The Moral Sense* (New York: Free Press, 1993).

14. See Harvey C. Mansfield and Delba Winthrop, "Liberalism and Big Government: Tocqueville's Analysis," unpublished paper.

Index

MAJOR CONCEPTS IN POLITICS
AND POLITICAL THEORY

This series invites book manuscripts and proposals on major concepts in politics and political theory—justice, equality, virtue, rights, citizenship, power, sovereignty, property, liberty, etc.—in prominent traditions, periods, and thinkers.

Send manuscripts or proposals, with author's vitae to:

Garrett Ward Sheldon
General Editor
College Avenue
Clinch Valley College
University Virginia
Wise, VA 24293